TABLE BY THE WINDOW

A Play in Three Scenes

It is the author's wish that in all future productions
Table by the Window and *Table Number Seven* should
be known as *Table No. 1* and *Table No. 2* respectively.

SEPARATE TABLES

Two Plays

by

TERENCE RATTIGAN

SAMUEL   FRENCH

LONDON
NEW YORK   TORONTO   SYDNEY   HOLLYWOOD

TABLE BY THE WINDOW

Produced at the St James's Theatre, London, on the 22nd September, 1954, with the following cast of characters:

(in the order of speaking)

MABEL	*Marion Fawcett*
LADY MATHESON	*Jane Eccles*
MRS RAILTON-BELL	*Phyllis Neilson-Terry*
MISS MEACHAM	*May Hallait*
DOREEN	*Priscilla Morgan*
MRS FOWLER	*Aubrey Mather*
MRS SHANKLAND	*Margaret Leighton*
MISS COOPER	*Beryl Measor*
MR MALCOLM	*Eric Portman*
MR STRATTON	*Basil Henson*
MISS TANNER	*Patricia Raine*

Directed by PETER GLENVILLE
Settings by MICHAEL WEIGHT

SYNOPSIS OF SCENES

The action of the Play takes place at the Beauregard Private Hotel, Bournemouth, during winter

SCENE I
The dining-room. Dinner time

SCENE II
The lounge. After dinner

SCENE III
The dining-room. The following morning

Time—the present

SCENE I

SCENE—*The dining-room of the Beauregard Private Hotel, Bournemouth. Dinner time on a winter's evening.*

It is a small room, rather bare and quite unpretentious, the upstage half being raised on a rostrum up two steps. A door LC of the back wall leads to the lounge and a baize, swing door up L leads to the kitchen. There is a large bay window with a window-seat across the corner up R. The fireplace is down L, and in the wall down R, there is a small built-in alcove with shelves. There are six separate tables with chairs and a double table up C with chairs R and L of it. Four of the separate tables are downstage, one R, one RC, one LC and one L. Two tables are on the rostrum, one up RC, near the window and the other LC.

(See the Ground Plan and Photograph of the Scene)

When the CURTAIN *rises, it is about 7 o'clock. The window curtains are closed and the lights and table-lamps are lit. The guests are at dinner. Each sits at a small separate table, except for a young couple,* MR CHARLES STRATTON *and* MISS JEAN TANNER *who, as mere transients, occupy a table together back C, not garnished, as are the other tables, with the bottles of medicine and favourite pickles and other idiosyncratic personal accessories of the permanent residents. Surprisingly, for they are an attractive looking pair,* CHARLES *and* JEAN *are paying no attention to each other at all, and each is avidly reading a book propped up on the flower vase between them.* JEAN *wears slacks. They are eating their sweet course. Prominently placed, sitting above the downstage table* RC, *and indeed a rather prominent looking person altogether, is* MRS RAILTON-BELL. *All the ladies, except Jean, always change "into something" for dinner, but* MRS RAILTON-BELL *always changes into something much grander than the others. All the ladies, except Jean, wear fur stoles, but* MRS RAILTON-BELL'S *is of mink. Not a good mink, it is true, but a genuine mink none the less. All the ladies, except Jean, wear some small items of jewellery, but* MRS RAILTON-BELL'S *are far less small than the others. She is eating her sweet course.* MISS MEACHAM *is seated above the upstage table* LC, *reading, very close to her upspectacled eyes, a copy of "Racing Up To Date". Although much the same age as Mrs Railton-Bell, about sixty-five, she is dressed in a far more sprightly fashion, but has not succeeded in looking any younger. She is just finishing her soup.* LADY MATHESON *is seated* R *of the table down* R. *She is a Civil Servant's widow living on an annuity and therefore the poorest of all the residents. She is a grey-faced, mousey, impeccably dressed woman, rather younger than the other two. She is finishing her soup.* MR FOWLER *is seated* R *of the table down* L. *He is an ex-public schoolmaster, seventyish, quiet and impassive-looking. He is drinking his soup. The table up* RC, *on the rostrum near the window is unoccupied, as is the downstage table* LC. *Two waitresses,* MABEL *and* DOREEN, *serve the guests.* MABEL *is middle-aged, taciturn, gloomy and dependable.* DOREEN *is young, flighty, talkative and undependable. At the moment only* MABEL *is visible. She is serving Lady Matheson at the table down* R *and has a tray with plates of Goulash and Medaillon and two dishes of vegetables.*

MABEL. Were you medaillon or goulash?
LADY MATHESON (*correctly accenting*) Medaillon.
MABEL. Sorry. I thought you were goulash.
LADY MATHESON. It was probably my fault.

(MRS RAILTON-BELL, *with a decorous gesture, puts her finger to her lips. There is silence.* MABEL *serves Lady Matheson*)

(*She smiles sweetly at Mabel*) I'm so sorry, Mabel, I'm quite sure it was I that made the mistake.
MABEL (*gloomily*) I dare say. (*She passes on to* L *of Miss Meacham*) You *were* goulash, weren't you, Miss Meacham?
MISS MEACHAM (*deep in her book*) What? Oh, yes, Mabel. Thank you.
MABEL. (*serving Miss Meacham with goulash*) And what to follow —the mousse angelic, or the turnover?
MISS MEACHAM. Which do you think?
MABEL. Turnover.
MISS MEACHAM. Turnover, then.

(*Mabel drifts away through the kitchen door up* L)

MRS RAILTON-BELL (*to Miss Meacham*) I think cook's acquiring a little lighter touch with her pastry, don't you think?
MISS MEACHAM. Not judging by the tarts we had at tea yesterday. Cannon balls. (*She eats her goulash*)
MRS RAILTON-BELL. Did you think so? I quite liked them. I much preferred them to those pink cakes on Tuesday.
MISS MEACHAM. I didn't mind the pink cakes. The tarts gave me the collywobbles. I had the most terrible dreams.
MRS RAILTON-BELL (*with a faint smile*) I thought you were always having dreams.
MISS MEACHAM. Oh, these weren't my proper dreams. Not the ones I make myself dream. These were just horrible, pointless nightmares. Cosh boys and things. (*After a slight pause*) I talked to Louis the Fifteenth on Thursday night.
MRS RAILTON-BELL (*plainly humouring her*) Did you indeed, dear?

Miss Meacham. The goulash's rather good. I think you made a mistake. (*She goes back to her book*)

(*There is a silence for a few moments while* Miss Meacham *peruses her "Racing Up to Date" with myopic concentration*)

Mrs Railton-Bell. Think you've found a winner for tomorrow, Miss Meacham?

Miss Meacham. "Marston Lad" is worth a bob or two each way.

Mrs Railton-Bell. I never bet nowadays. (*She pours some wine into her glass. After a meditative pause*) When my husband was alive he used sometimes to put as much as five pounds on a horse for me.

Miss Meacham. I used to bet in ponies when my father was alive, and I had an allowance. (*She goes back to her book*) Well —if the form . . .

Mrs Railton-Bell (*suddenly irritable*) Why don't you get spectacles?

Miss Meacham (*lowering her book*) Because I don't need them. (*She goes back to her book*)

(Doreen *enters from the kitchen. She carries a tray with a plate of tongue and salad, moves to* l *of Fowler and hovers over him*)

Doreen. Sorry, Mr Fowler, the goulash's off.

(Fowler *looks up abstractedly*)

Fowler. What? Oh. (*He looks at the menu*) What about the cold pie?

Doreen. I shouldn't have that, if I were you. I saw what went into it. If I were you I'd have this tongue. *H>tvy*

Fowler. All right. Whatever you say.

(Doreen *takes Fowler's soup plate, gives him the tongue, crosses to Mrs Railton-Bell, and collects her plate*)

Doreen. Ta.

(Doreen *exits to the kitchen*)

Mrs Railton-Bell (*to Lady Matheson; meaningly*) She won't last.

Lady Matheson. I'm afraid not.

Mrs Railton-Bell. Still, it's disgraceful that the goulash's off, and two people not even in yet.

Lady Matheson. I know.

Mrs Railton-Bell. Of course, Mr Malcolm's never on time— (*she indicates the table by the window*) and really deserves it. (*In another confidential whisper*) Anyway, after those long sessions at the *Feathers* I often wonder if he ever really knows what he's eating. But the new lady—(*she indicates the table* LC) I mean, my dear, what will she think?

LADY MATHESON. I saw her arrive.

MRS RAILTON-BELL. Did you?

LADY MATHESON. Yes—did you?

MRS RAILTON-BELL (*slightly annoyed*) I was in the lounge, but I didn't—excuse me—think it quite the thing to peer out of the window at her . . .

LADY MATHESON (*firmly*) I happened to be in the hall.

MISS MEACHAM. I met her on the stairs.

MRS RAILTON-BELL. Really, dear?

MISS MEACHAM (*still absorbed in her book*) She's called Mrs Shankland. She comes from London, she arrived by train, she has four suitcases and a hatbox and she's staying two weeks.

MRS RAILTON-BELL (*unwillingly impressed*) Four suitcases?

MISS MEACHAM. And a hatbox.

LADY MATHESON. She was awfully smartly dressed. Nothing flashy—very good taste—but—well —Mayfair, if you know what I mean.

MRS RAILTON-BELL. Really? (*She picks up the menu and changes the subject from this unwelcome topic*) It was quite nice out this afternoon, didn't you think, dear—I mean, for December.

LADY MATHESON. I didn't go out, I'm afraid. There was a Sibelius concert on the Home . . .

MRS RAILTON-BELL. You and your music. Did you go out, Mr Fowler?

FOWLER. What? No, I didn't. I was waiting for a telephone call.

MRS RAILTON-BELL. I was the only brave one then? Fancy. I always say the weather in December . . .

(MRS RAILTON-BELL *breaks off abruptly as the door up* LC *opens.*

MRS SHANKLAND, ANNE, *the new arrival, enters up* LC. *She is about forty, and, as she stands just inside the room looking around rather timidly, she seems entirely out of place in such an environment. Not that her clothes are unsuitable, although they are smart, nor that her coiffure is too stylish, although it is stylish, but that she has brought on with her an air of Belgravia and the smarter London restaurants. She stands now as if waiting for a head waiter to guide her to her table. None of the other guests glance at her.*

MABEL *enters from the kitchen. She carries a tray with a turnover for Miss Meacham*)

MABEL (*to Anne*) You're the new one, aren't you?

ANNE. Yes.

MABEL (*indicating the table* LC) You're here.

ANNE. Oh. Thank you. (*She goes to the table* LC, *sits and studies the menu*)

(*Dead silence still reigns.* Mabel *moves to Miss Meacham, serves her with the turnover, then moves to Anne. The other guests begin to cast quick, furtive glances in Anne's direction*)

Mabel (*to Anne*) The brown windsor or the petite marmite?
Anne. I don't think I'll have any soup, thank you. I'll try the goulash.
Mabel. That's right. We've got a portion left.

(Fowler *bangs his fork down and glares furiously at Mabel, but decides not to make a scene.*
Mabel *exits to the kitchen. Eyes are lowered again as* Anne *looks curiously around the room. The silence continues until it is at length broken by* Mrs Railton-Bell, *speaking now in a rather louder and more self-consciously well-bred voice than before*)

Mrs Railton-Bell (*to Lady Matheson; peeling her apple*) I was saying about the weather in December . . .
Lady Matheson. Oh, yes?
Mrs Railton-Bell. It can be so treacherous, especially here, on the south coast. This afternoon, for instance, even though the sun was quite bright, I put on a fur coat—my warmest one, too—the Persian Lamb . . .
Lady Matheson. Very sensible of you.

(Charles *and* Jean *rise abruptly and exit up* lc *to the lounge, each carrying their book. They have still, as far as we can see, not addressed a word to each other.* Mrs Railton-Bell *eyes them with disdain*)

Mrs Railton-Bell. Trousers at dinner!
Lady Matheson. I know.
Mrs Railton-Bell. And he never changes either. I wonder Miss Cooper doesn't say something. You'd think they'd teach them better manners at Oxford.
Lady Matheson. Yes, you would. (*After a slight pause*) My husband was at Oxford.
Mrs Railton-Bell (*gently*) Yes, dear, You've told me so before. Mine only went to Birmingham because of the wonderful engineering course they have there.

(Miss Cooper *enters up* lc *and moves to Anne.* Miss Cooper *is youngish, with a rather masculine appearance and a quiet manner*)

He hated it, of course.
Miss Cooper (*pausing*) Good evening, Mrs Railton-Bell. Good evening. Lady Matheson.
Mrs Railton-Bell. Good evening, Miss Cooper.
Lady Matheson. Good evening.

(MISS MEACHAM *does not look up*.

MABEL *enters from the kitchen. She carries a tray with Anne's goulash, moves to* L *of the table and serves Anne.* MISS COOPER *continues her journey towards Anne's table*)

MISS COOPER (R *of Anne*) Is everything all right, Mrs Shankland?

ANNE. Yes, thank you.

MISS COOPER. I'm so sorry I wasn't here to show you your table. I had a telephone call from London. Are you being looked after all right?

ANNE. Yes, thank you.

(MABEL *exits to the kitchen*)

MISS COOPER (*sharply*) No soup?

ANNE. No. I don't care for it. It's bad for the figure.

MISS COOPER. I shouldn't have thought you'd have to worry about that, Mrs Shankland.

ANNE (*pouring herself a glass of water*) Oh, I do. I work at modelling, you know.

MISS COOPER. And now you're down here for a little rest?

ANNE. Yes. That's right.

MISS COOPER. I hope you find your room quite comfortable.

ANNE. I'm sure I shall.

MISS COOPER. If there's anything you want, please don't hesitate to ask me.

ANNE. I won't.

(MABEL *enters from the kitchen. She carries a tray with a turnover for Lady Matheson.* MISS COOPER *flashes Anne a cordial smile, extinguished instantly as she turns away to the table up* RC. MABEL *removes Lady Matheson's plate and serves her with the turnover.* MISS COOPER *glances at the empty table and summons Mabel with a gesture*)

MISS COOPER. Mabel——

MABEL. Yes, miss?

MISS COOPER. —go to Mr Malcolm's room and tell . . .

MABEL. I've been. He's not there.

MISS COOPER. Oh. Have they kept something hot for him?

MABEL. Yes but Cook says if he's not in in five minutes he'll have to have cold.

MISS COOPER. Oh, well, I don't expect he'll be more than that.

(MABEL *looks unconvinced and exits to the kitchen.* MISS COOPER *stands by the window* R)

FOWLER. Miss Cooper! Did I hear you say something about a telephone call?

MISS COOPER. I'm afraid it wasn't from your guest, Mr Fowler.

It was from Major Pollock. He wanted to leave a new forwarding address.

Mrs Railton-Bell. Ringing up from London? That's very extravagant—for the Major.

Miss Cooper (*with a faint smile*) He was calling from a friend's house, I gather. He's coming back next Tuesday he says.

Miss Meacham (*through her book*) Oh, God! That old bore.

(Miss Cooper *straightens the window curtains, then crosses to* Fowler, *who rises and moves to the door up* LC. Miss Cooper *helps* Fowler *up the steps and then stands* R *of him*)

Fowler. I can't understand Philip not ringing up. How can he expect to be met at the station if we don't know what train . . .

Miss Cooper. Have you tried ringing him?

Fowler. Yes. Twice. No answer either time. Perhaps I'd better try again. (*He goes through the change in his pocket*)

Miss Cooper. It's a little late, Mr Fowler. There's only one train left from London.

Fowler (*at the door*) Please don't worry about the room, Miss Cooper. If anything's gone wrong—which I don't believe mind you—I'll pay for it, I promise you.

Miss Cooper. That won't be necessary, Mr Fowler. But I *would* rather like to know—if you don't mind—as soon as possible.

(Fowler *exits up* LC. Miss Cooper *picks up the vase from the table up* C, *crosses to Fowler's table down* L *and picks up the vase from it*)

Mrs Railton-Bell (*sympathetically*) It's too bad, Miss Cooper. This is the third time, isn't it?

Miss Cooper. I expect he'll turn up. Just forgotten to phone, that's all. You know what these Bohemian young people are like.

(Miss Cooper *exits to the kitchen*)

Mrs Railton-Bell (*to Lady Matheson*) I don't, as it happens. I don't care for Bohemians. (*In her confidential whisper*) We have one too many here, I should have thought. (*With her head she indicates the table by the window*) And I'm beginning to doubt the very existence of Mr Fowler's famous young painter friend.

Lady Matheson. I know he exists. Mr Fowler showed me an article on him in *Picture Post*. He was the head boy of Mr Fowler's house at Tonbridge, I gather. So proud of him, Mr Fowler is—it's really quite touching to hear him go on.

Mrs Railton-Bell. Well, I think it's a disgrace that he keeps on letting him down like this.

Miss Meacham (*suddenly closing her book*) Nonsense!

Mrs Railton-Bell (*startled*) What, dear?

Miss Meacham. It's not a disgrace at all. (*She puts down her book and folds her napkin*) Why should we old has-beens expect the young to show us considerations? We've had our life. They've still got theirs to live. Seeing us can only remind them of death, and old people's diseases. I've got two of the prettiest nieces you ever saw. You've seen their photographs in my room. But they never come near me, and I wouldn't like it if they did. (*She rises and picks up her book*) God knows I don't want to remind them of what they've got to become.

(MISS MEACHAM *exits up* LC)

MRS RAILTON-BELL (*to Lady Matheson; in her confidential whisper*) I'm getting a little worried about Miss Meacham.

LADY MATHESON. She's certainly getting more and more—unusual, every day.

MRS RAILTON-BELL. These dream-games of hers. (*She folds her napkin*) Well, I suppose they're harmless—but I really don't know what a psychiatrist would say. The human mind, you know—it's a very delicate piece of machinery—as my husband used to say—and—one never knows. Well—(*she rise majestically*) shall I see you in the lounge, or have you a date with the Third Programme?

LADY MATHESON. No. There's nothing worth hearing on to-night.

MRS RAILTON-BELL. Good. *A toute à l' heure,* then.

(MRS RAILTON-BELL. *sweeps regally out up* LC. LADY MATHESON *is now on her sweet.* ANNE *has finished toying with her goulash. Deep silence reigns.*

MABEL *enters from the kitchen. She carries a tray with a turnover for Anne*)

MABEL (*moving to* L *of Anne*) I've brought you the turnover. It's better than the other. (*She removes Anne's plate and serves her with the turnover*)

ANNE. Oh. Thank you so much.

(MABEL *exits to the kitchen. Once more silence reigns, then the door up* LC *is pushed open rather violently.*

JOHN MALCOLM *enters up* LC. *He is in the early forties, of rather rugged appearance, untidily dressed, and with unruly hair. When he speaks it will be with a slight north country accent. He looks quickly at his watch, and then at the kitchen door.* ANNE *sees John before he sees her, and stares at him, remotely, with no change of expression.* JOHN, *conscious of the stare, looks in Anne's direction and then stops dead* C, *his back to the audience. After a moment he walks on to the table by the window, and takes his seat, which is facing Anne's. He stares at the tablecloth.*

DOREEN *enters from the kitchen with an empty tray, to clear Miss Meacham's table*)

DOREEN (*to John*) Oh. You in at last? Thank heavens. I thought we'd never get off. (*She moves to the table up* LC *and clears it*) Where you been? *The Feathers?*

JOHN. Yes.

DOREEN. Thought so. The goulash's off. You'll have to have medaillon.

JOHN (*still staring at the tablecloth*) That's all right.

DOREEN. Brown windsor, like usual?

JOHN. Yes.

(DOREEN *exits to the kitchen. There is silence between the three. Finally,* LADY MATHESON *finishes, folds her napkin and rises*)

LADY MATHESON (*to Anne*) Good evening.

(LADY MATHESON *exits up* LC.
DOREEN *enters from the kitchen. She carries a tray with a plate of soup for John*)

DOREEN (*crossing and putting the plate in front of John*) There you are. Tuck into that. Not but what I wouldn't expect you've had enough liquid tonight already.

(DOREEN *exits to the kitchen.* JOHN *crumbles a piece of bread, and then slowly lifts his eyes from the tablecloth*)

JOHN (*at length*) Is this coincidence?

ANNE. Of course.

JOHN. What are you doing here?

ANNE. A rest-cure.

JOHN. Why this place—of all places?

ANNE. It was recommended to me.

JOHN. Who by?

ANNE. A man I met at a party somewhere.

JOHN. He didn't tell you I was here?

ANNE. No—he said something about a journalist—called John Malcolm. Is that you?

JOHN. Yes.

ANNE. Oh, yes, of course, I see. Your Christian names.

JOHN (savagely) Why, for the love of God, didn't you go to the *Royal Bath* or the *Branksome Towers,* or any of the grand hotels?

(DOREEN *enters from the kitchen with an empty tray, and clears the table up* C)

DOREEN (*to John*) What you having after, 'cause Cook's got to leave it out. Turnover is best.

JOHN. All right.

DOREEN. Finished your soup? (*She moves to John's table*)

JOHN. Yes, thank you.

DOREEN. You haven't touched it. (*She picks up his soup plate*) I *said* too much liquid . . .

(DOREEN *exits to the kitchen*)

ANNE. I couldn't afford a grand hotel.

JOHN. He pays you alimony, doesn't he?

ANNE. Seven-fifty a year. I don't find it very easy. You see, I'm not getting work these days.

JOHN. I thought he was a rich man.

ANNE. Michael? Oh, no. His antique shop lost a lot of money.

JOHN. He gets his name in the papers a lot.

ANNE. Oh, yes. Quite a social figure—first nights and all that.

JOHN. How long exactly were you married to him?

ANNE. Three years and six months.

JOHN. Beating me by three months? I saw the headlines of the case. They were quite juicy—but not as juicy as ours—you'll admit. It was cruelty again, wasn't it?

ANNE. Yes.

JOHN. Did *he* try to kill you, too?

ANNE (*quietly*) No.

(DOREEN *enters from the kitchen. She carries a tray with medaillon and vegetables for John*)

DOREEN. There you are. Usual veg?

(JOHN *nods*)

(*She serves John*) You look a bit down in the dumps tonight. Anything the matter?

JOHN. No.

DOREEN. All right. Don't take too long, will you? My friend's waiting.

(DOREEN *exits to the kitchen.* JOHN *makes no attempt to touch his food*)

JOHN. How did he show *his* cruelty?

ANNE. In lots of ways. Small ways. They can all be summed up by saying that he doesn't really like women.

JOHN. Why did he marry you?

ANNE. He wanted a wife.

JOHN. And you wanted a husband.

(ANNE *nods*)

As wide a contrast as possible from your first, I suppose. Still, couldn't you have done a bit better for yourself?

ANNE. I suppose so. But he was gentle and kind and made me laugh and I was fond of him. I went into it with my eyes well open. I thought I could make it work. I was wrong.

(JOHN *laughs suddenly*)

What's the joke?

JOHN. A nice poser for a woman's magazine. Girls, which husband would you choose? One who loves you too little—or one who loves you loves too much? (*After a pause*) Third time lucky, perhaps.
ANNE. Perhaps.

(*There is a pause*)

JOHN. How long are you staying here?
ANNE. I booked for two weeks.
JOHN. I'll go to London.
ANNE. No. If you feel like that, then I'll go to another hotel.
JOHN. That might be easier.

(*There is a pause*)

ANNE. John—I don't see why . . .
JOHN. Do you think these old women don't notice anything? They spend their whole days gossiping. They know I write in the *New Outlook* under the name of Cato—and how they found that out I'll never know, because none of them would sully their dainty fingers by even touching such a Bolshie rag.
ANNE. I read it every week.
JOHN. Turning left-wing in your old age?
ANNE (*quietly*) My old age?
JOHN. How old are you now?
ANNE. Well—let's just say eight years older than when I last saw you.
JOHN. Yes. You don't look it.
ANNE. Thank you. But I feel it.

(*There is a pause*)

JOHN. Why didn't you come to see me in prison yourself?
ANNE. I wanted to. I was stopped.
JOHN. Who by?
ANNE. My mother and father.
JOHN. I suppose they told you I might try to strangle you in front of the warder. I nearly did try to strangle your solicitor.
ANNE. They thought it would make it easier for you if I kept away.
JOHN. A very well-bred, Christian thought. My dear ex-in-laws. How are they?
ANNE. My father's dead. My mother lives in a place rather like this, in Kensington.

(*There is a pause.* JOHN *rises and crosses to* R *of Anne's table*)

JOHN (*at length*) Then you'll go tomorrow, will you?
ANNE. Yes.
JOHN. Thank you. (*Stiffly*) I'm sorry to have to put you to so much inconvenience.
ANNE. That's all right.

(JOHN *moves abruptly towards the door up* LC)

John.

JOHN (*coming back to her*) What do we do now—shake hands?

(ANNE *rises and goes up to John, then puts her hnds on his shoulders and kisses him gently on the cheek*)

ANNE. I'm very glad to see you again, John.

JOHN (*putting her hands away from him*) It may seem boorisn of me not to be able to say the same, Anne. But then I am a boor, as you know. In fact, you must still have a scar on the side of your head to prove it to you.

ANNE. It's gone now.

JOHN. Gone? After five stitches and a week in hospital?

ANNE. Eight years will cure most scars.

JOHN. Most, I suppose. Not all, though. Well, good night. (*He goes towards the door up* LC)

(ANNE *resumes her seat and takes her compact from her handbag.*

MISS COOPER *enters up* LC)

MISS COOPER. Oh, good evening, Mr Malcolm.

JOHN. Good evening. (*He makes a move to pass her*)

MISS COOPER. Did you want something? Is there anything I can do for you?

JOHN. I've finished, thank you. I'm going out.

MISS COOPER. Oh. (*With a hint of anxiety*) It's a horrible night, you know. It's started to pour . . .

JOHN. It doesn't matter.

(JOHN *exits up* LC)

MISS COOPER (*following John*) I'll have to open the door for you. I'd already locked up. (*To Anne*) Excuse me, Mrs Shankland.

(MISS COOPER *exits up* LC. ANNE, *left alone, looks thoughtfully at herself in her compact mirror for a long time.*

MISS COOPER *re-enters up* LC. ANNE *closes her compact and replaces it in her bag*)

(*She moves to* R *of Anne*) Coffee is served in the lounge, Mrs Shankland. I thought, when you've finished your dinner, you might like me to take you in there and introduce you to some of your fellow-guests. People are sometimes so odd about not talking to newcomers, I don't know why, and I hate any of my guests to feel lonely. (*Conversationally*) Loneliness is a terrible thing, don't you agree?

ANNE. Yes, I do agree. A terrible thing. (*She picks up her handbag*)

MISS COOPER. Oh. Have you finished? Good. Then let's go in,

shall we? (*She indicates the door up* L.C) The lounge is through here. (*She holds the door open*)

Anne (*rising and moving to the door up* LC) Thank you.

Anne *exits up* LC *as the lights dim and—*

the Curtain *falls*

SCENE II

SCENE—*The lounge. After dinner.*

The room has french windows across the corner up L. The door to the dining-room is up two steps RC of the back wall. An arch up R leads to the entrance hall and other parts of the hotel. The fireplace, with a gas fire and club fender is down R. A single-ended sofa stands at an angle LC. There is an easy chair above the fireplace and a fireside chair below it. An armchair stands RC and a small chair, facing up stage is L of the sofa. There is a settee L, a small table down R and a pouffe RC. A writing-desk and chair is R of the french windows and a table for magazines is C of the back wall. At night the room is lit by wall-brackets over the fireplace and two standard lamps, one behind the settee L and one R of the desk.
(See the Ground Plan and Photograph of the Scene)

When the CURTAIN *rises, the lights and gas fire are lit, the window curtains are closed and the rain can be heard beating against the windows.* CHARLES *and* JEAN *are the only two residents in the room, and both are reading intently.* CHARLES *is lying on the sofa.* JEAN *is seated on the chair LC, with her back to the audience.*

CHARLES (*breaking a long silence; into his book*) There's going to be a storm.

JEAN. Hell! I hate spray. (*She turns round in her chair and sits astride it, facing front*)

CHARLES (*after another silence*) Where are they all?

JEAN. The new one's gone up to her room. So has old Dreamgirl. The Bournemouth Belle and Minnie Mouse are in the television room. Karl Marx is out boozing, and Mr Chips is still ringing up his painter friend.

CHARLES. He won't come.

JEAN. Of course he won't. (*She closes her book, rises and stretches herself*) I've finished my *Stubbs*. (*She puts the book on the pouffe*) How are you doing with your anatomy?

CHARLES. I'd do better if you'd shut up.

JEAN (*crossing above the sofa to L of him*) I didn't start the small talk. You did. Does your father know about me?

CHARLES (*making a note*) Yes.

JEAN. What did you tell him?

CHARLES. What?

(JEAN *kneels* L *of the sofa, over Charles' legs and pushes his book against his lap, preventing him from reading*)

JEAN. What did you tell him?

CHARLES. Don't do that, Jean. I'm in the middle of the trickiest duct in the whole human body.

JEAN. What did you tell him?

CHARLES (*angrily*) Oh, for God's sake—that we were in love with each other and going to get married, of course. (*He pulls the book back and furrows his brows over it again*)

JEAN (*leaning forward*) You told him a dirty lie, then, didn't you—I mean about us going to get married.

CHARLES. What? Oh, yes. I had to put it like that, otherwise he wouldn't have understood. Now shut up for God's sake.

(CHARLES *allows* JEAN *to take the book from him*)

JEAN. You'd better stop now. If you go on much longer you know you won't sleep, and it'll make you old before your time.

CHARLES. I suppose you're right.

(JEAN *throws the book on to the pouffe*)

Don't lose the place. (*He stretches*) My God—to be old before one's time. What a fate! I wonder if all old people are as miserable as these?

JEAN (*sitting on the downstage end of the sofa, facing front*) They're not miserable. Look at old Dream-girl. She's as happy as a sand-girl communing with her spirits and waiting for the racing results. The Bournemouth Belle's quite happy, too, queening it around here in her silver fox and with her daughter to look after her.

CHARLES. Has she got a daughter?

JEAN (*playing with his socks and suspenders*) Don't you listen to anything? She never stops trilling away about her dear Sibyl, and how they're really more like good pals than mother and daughter, and how dear Sibyl can't live without her.

CHARLES. You mean the daughter lives with her here? My God, what a fate! I haven't seen her.

JEAN. She's escaped for a couple of weeks, I gather, to an aunt. Anyway, the Bournemouth Belle's too self-centred an old brute to be anything but happy. Minnie Mouse *is* a bit grey and depressed, I grant. But she's got her music, and Mr Chips has got his ex-pupils, even if he doesn't ever see them. As for Karl Marx—well . . .

CHARLES. Now you can't say Karl Marx isn't miserable. I've never seen a more miserable-looking wreck.

JEAN. Oh, I don't know. He's got his booze and his articles in the *New Outlook* and his vague air of a murky past, and his hints of former glories. (*She turns round and lies on his stomach, looking at him. With seriousness*) No, Charles. Do you know who I think is the only one in this hotel who really *is* miserable?

CHARLES. Miss Cooper?

JEAN (*scornfully*) Miss Cooper! No. She's as gay as a bee pinning up her notices in the bathroom and being generally managerial. No. I meant the new one.

CHARLES. Mrs Shankland? But you've only met her for a second an hour ago.

JEAN. A woman can't fool another woman just with a pretty dress and a gay manner and a bright smile. (*She turns on her back and lies with her head on his chest*) She's been through some form of hell, that creature. Anyway, what's she doing down here? Dressed like that and looking like that she ought to be at the *Royal Bath*, or something. Besides—she's not wearing a wedding ring.

CHARLES. Really, Jean, you're getting as bad as the old girls. Perhaps it's got broken or something.

JEAN. She's divorced—that I'm sure of.

CHARLES. Well, all right. So she's divorced. Does that make her a tragic figure? I would have thought, according to your ideas on marriage, it ought to make her a happy one.

JEAN (*rising*) My ideas on marriage are only for us, Charles, because I'm going to have a career and you're going to be a famous surgeon and don't want hordes of children cluttering up your consulting room. (*She collects the books from the pouffe*) But other people aren't as sensible as we are. They go and get married, then they get miserable when it goes wrong. (*She moves to the chair* LC *and puts her left knee on it*) Thank heavens that can't happen to us. We're too integrated. At least I am, I know, and I hope you are, too.

CHARLES. Come and give me a kiss and I'll show you how integrated I am.

JEAN. I'd only put lipstick on your collar and the old girls will notice.

CHARLES. Sometimes, Jean darling, I'm not sure I wouldn't like to see to you, just ever so slightly, disintegrate. (*He rises, strides over and kisses her*)

(JEAN *appears quite to enjoy the embrace. There is the sound of voices in the hall*)

Oh blast!

JEAN (*levelly*) Wipe your mouth.

CHARLES. Damn it all, even the old girls know the facts of life.

JEAN. They may know them, but they don't like them.

(CHARLES *takes his handkerchief from his pocket and wipes his mouth.*
    MRS RAILTON-BELL *and* LADY MATHESON *enter up* R. MRS RAILTON-BELL *carries a copy of the "Radio Times". She notices Charles' handkerchief*)

Mrs Railton-Bell (*as she enters*) Yes, wasn't he splendid. He completely floored that horrid Socialist. (*To Jean and Charles. Coldly*) Hullo. Finished your work? (*She puts her paper on the table up* c)

(Lady Matheson *moves to the fireplace*)

Jean ⎫ (*together*) ⎧Yes.
Charles ⎭   ⎩Yes, we have. Just going to bed.
Mrs Railton-Bell. Good night.

(Jean *crosses below the pouffe towards the arch up* R. Charles *crosses above the sofa to the arch up* R)

Jean ⎫ (*together*) ⎧Good night, Mrs Railton-Bell. Good
Charles ⎭   ⎨ night, Lady Matheson.
                    ⎩Good night. See you at breakfast.

(Charles *exits up* R.

Jean, *balancing the books on her head, follows him off*)

Mrs Railton-Bell (*moving* R *of the sofa*) They've been making love.

Lady Matheson (*sitting in the chair down* R) How do you know?

Mrs Railton-Bell (*moving to the easy chair above the fireplace*) The look in their eyes. And just as I came in he was putting a handkerchief away with lipstick marks on it.

Lady Matheson. Well, perhaps they *are* in love. I always thought there must be something.

Mrs Railton-Bell (*sitting in the easy chair*) But they're supposed to have come here just to work. Old friends and all that. That's what they told Miss Cooper. If they're in love, why don't they say so? I hate something furtive. What were we saying?

Lady Matheson. About the man on television being so good.

Mrs Railton-Bell. Oh, yes. Now what was it he said that was so true . . .

(*The french windows are opened from the outside and the curtains are blown violently inwards*)

Good gracious!

(John, *after a moment's battling with the billowing curtains, enters by the french windows. He is wearing a drenched raincoat. He appears to have had quite a few drinks*)

Please close that at once. There's the most terrible draught.

John. A draught? Oh, yes. (*He disappears behind the curtains*)

(Mrs Railton-Bell *exchanges a speaking glance with* Lady Matheson, *and frames the word "drunk" with her lips*)

Lady Matheson. Yes. Now what was it he said? So telling. Something about the national cake.

(JOHN's *struggle to close the french windows are concluded.
He emerges and, still in his raincoat, moves to the chair* LC *and
sits, leaning forward. The two ladies look at him, and* MRS
RAILTON-BELL *decides to ignore his presence*)

MRS RAILTON-BELL. Yes. I remember now. It was in that
wonderful answer he gave about levelling up rather than levelling
down.

(JOHN *clears his throat*)

He said, don't you remember that whereas the Socialists were
only concerned about cutting the national cake into exactly
equal slices, the Conservatives were trying to increase the size of
the cake.

(JOHN *clears his throat*)

(*She glances at* John) And then he said that every wage increase
meant a smaller cake for cutting . . .
JOHN (*abruptly*) Who said this?
MRS RAILTON-BELL. Sir Roger Williamson, on television.
JOHN. I might have guessed it.
MRS RAILTON-BELL (*bristling*) I gather you don't agree with
what he said, Mr Malcolm?
JOHN (*looking round at them*) Of course I don't agree. You
know damn well I don't agree. That's not the point. They've got
some clever people in that party. Why do they have to put an old
ass like that on television—(*he leans over the back of his chair*)
with a falsetto voice, a face like an angry walrus and the mind of
a backward child of eight?
MRS RAILTON-BELL. That was *not our* impression of Sir Roger.
JOHN. Poor old Roger. I suppose he needs the dough to make a
little back on what he spends on all those girl friends of his.
MRS RAILTON-BELL (*after a moment's appalled silence*) Do I
understand that you are personally acquainted with Sir Roger, Mr
Malcolm?

(JOHN *rises, and as he speaks, moves to the table up* C *and
picks up a magazine*)

JOHN. No. Never met him.
MRS RAILTON-BELL. Then may I ask by what right . . . ?
JOHN (*looking at the magazine*) No right. I just hear things,
that's all.
MRS RAILTON-BELL. Some very libellous things, if I may say so.
JOHN. Yes, the greater the truth the greater the libel is the
phrase, isn't it? (*He pauses, during which he crosses to the settee*
L *and sits*) What else did Sir Roger say? Did he mention the go-
slow in the docks?
MRS RAILTON-BELL. Yes. As a matter of fact, he did. He said

that the dock workers seemed to have no sense of national responsibility . . .

JOHN. There's no body of men in England with more.

MRS RAILTON-BELL. That's no doubt something else that you have *heard*, Mr Malcolm.

JOHN. No. That's something I *know*. I used to be a docker myself.

(*There is a pause*)

MRS RAILTON-BELL (*at length*) I am not, if I may say so, at all surprised to hear it.

JOHN (*rising and moving* L *of the sofa*) And I am not surprised you're not surprised, Mrs Railton-Bell. (*He burps gently*) Excuse me. Too much whisky.

(MRS RAILTON-BELL *and* LADY MATHESON *exchange a glance.* JOHN *intercepts it*)

Keeps the cold out, you know. (*He throws the magazine on to the desk*) I gather you two ladies read the *New Outlook?*

MRS RAILTON-BELL. I certainly never do any such thing. I wouldn't soil my hands.

JOHN (*leaning over the sofa*) That's just what I thought. Do you, Lady Matheson?

LADY MATHESON. I have glanced at it on occasions, yes. (*Hastily*) Not for the political side, of course, but it has very good music criticism.

JOHN. So it was you who found out I was Cato, was it? Smart of you. How did you guess?

LADY MATHESON (*confused*) If you must know, you left some typescript lying about on that table over there. I picked it up, not knowing what is was, and read just the opening paragraph, no more, but it was enough for me to recognize it in print a week or so later.

JOHN. I see. My fault, then. No ill-feelings—on this side, any-way. (*He burps again*) Excuse me. What was the article on? (*He sits on the upstage end of the sofa, with his back to the audience*)

LADY MATHESON. Dividends and wages.

JOHN. Did you read it all?

LADY MATHESON. Yes, I did.

JOHN. What did you think of it?

LADY MATHESON (*with unusual spirit*) Since you ask, I thought it was monstrous—utterly monstrous. I very nearly wrote you a letter about it.

JOHN. I wish you had. I enjoy controversy. You must have taken it a bit personally, I'm afraid.

LADY MATHESON. And how else could I take it? Do you realize that I have to live on a little less than half of what the average dock-worker makes a year? My husband was in the Civil Service and died before the pension scheme came into force. Still, the sum he left me seemed perfectly adequate at the time. And now . . .

JOHN. I know. You can't afford to have your wireless repaired—and you live by it. You had to move into a small back room when they raised the hotel prices last year. You can only afford one cinema a week, in the front rows. I bet you don't even buy the *New Outlook*—you borrow it. In short, by any reasonable standards you're well below the poverty line, and, as the poor have always had our passionate sympathy, Lady Matheson, you have mine.

LADY MATHESON. Thank you, but I can do very well without it.

JOHN. I wonder if you can. You're the unlucky victims of our revolution—you and Miss Meacham and Mr Fowler and the others. You should appeal to our humane instincts, Lady Matheson.

LADY MATHESON. By voting for your side, I suppose?

JOHN. That would be the most practical way, I agree.

LADY MATHESON (*staunchly*) Never! Never till I die.

MRS RAILTON-BELL. Your humane instincts! Tell me, why didn't you mention *me* just now, when you were talking of victims?

JOHN. Because you're not one, and won't be either, until our capital levy gets at that tidy little nest egg of yours.

MRS RAILTON-BELL (*to Lady Matheson; utterly outraged*) I think we should go, Gladys, and leave Mr Malcolm down here to sleep it off. (*She rises*)

JOHN. Oh, are you leaving, ladies? I mustn't forget my manners must I? (*He gets up with slight difficulty*) I've enjoyed our little chat. Don't forget, next election—vote Labour.

(LADY MATHESON *rises and looks in her chair for her glasses*)

MRS RAILTON-BELL (*moving to the arch up* R) It's our own fault, Gladys. We should never have allowed ourselves to be drawn into an argument with a drunken Red.

(MRS RAILTON-BELL *has plainly intended this as an exit line, but her exit is delayed because* LADY MATHESON *is feverishly searching.* LADY MATHESON *moves to the table up* C *and looks on it. As she does so,* JOHN *raises the cushion on the sofa.* LADY MATHESON *returns to her chair down* R)

(*Impatiently*) Come along, Gladys.

LADY MATHESON. I've left my reading glasses somewhere.

(MISS COOPER *enters from the dining-room. She carries a tray with coffee for one*)

MISS COOPER (*brightly*) Here you are, Mrs Railton-Bell. I'm not too late, I hope?

MRS RAILTON-BELL (*with heavy meaning*) Thank you, Miss

Cooper, but I'm not having my coffee tonight. (*To Lady Matheson Impatiently*) Can't you find them, dear?

(Miss Cooper *quickly takes in the scene and stares coldly at John*)

Lady Matheson. I'll just have another look in my ~~chair.~~ *BAG* (*She finds her glasses*) ~~Here they are.~~

Miss Cooper (*moving above the sofa; in a very managerial voice*) Mr Malcolm, did you come in through the french windows? *by the garden door.*

John (*humbly*) Yes, I did.

Miss Cooper. You know that there's a hotel rule against that?

John. I'd forgotten it. I'm very sorry.

Miss Cooper. There's mud all over the floor—oh, really! (~~*She puts the coffee tray on the pouffe and moves to L of the chair LC*~~) And you've been sitting in this chair with your wet mackintosh on.

John. I'm very sorry.

Miss Cooper. I must ask you if you would be so kind as to take your mackintosh off and hang it up in the proper place. Also to wipe your shoes on the mat provided for that purpose.

John. Yes. I'm very sorry.

(John *crosses and staggers off up* R. Mrs Railton-Bell *draws aside as he staggers past her*)

Miss Cooper (*moving a step up; anxiously*) Has there been a little bother?

Mrs Railton-Bell. A little bother is a distinct understatement.

Miss Cooper. Oh, dear! What was it?

Mrs Railton-Bell. I would prefer not to discuss it now. (*Very impatiently*) For heaven's sake come along, Gladys. That dreadful man may be back at any moment.

Lady Matheson (*moving to* R *of Mrs Railton-Bell; triumphantly*) Ah! They were ~~underneath the chair.~~ *in my bag.*

Mrs Railton-Bell. I can't think why you didn't look there in the first place.

(Miss Cooper *kneels and picks up some mud from the carpet by the desk and puts it in the waste-paper basket*)

~~Lady Matheson. Well, I was sitting in Mr Fowler's chair after dinner, you see, as the new lady was sitting in mine, quite inadvertently, I'm sure, and I thought . . .~~

Mrs Railton-Bell. ~~It doesn't matter, dear. Go along now.~~ Quick. (*She shoos Lady Matheson off* R)

(Lady Matheson *exits up* R)

(*She turns to Miss Cooper*) I should like to see you tomorrow morning after breakfast, Miss Cooper. Good night.

Miss Cooper. Good night, Mrs Railton-Bell.

(MRS RAILTON-BELL *exits up* R)

MRS RAILTON-BELL (*off*) Good night, Mr Fowler.

(MISS COOPER *rises, sighs, closes the dining-room door, collects the cushion from the chair* LC, *crosses to the fireplace, sits on the fender and dries the cushion at the fire.*

FOWLER *enters up* R)

FOWLER. Ah, there you are, Miss Cooper. (*He crosses to the desk and takes a sheet of writing paper and an envelope from it*) I've come for some notepaper.
MISS COOPER. Any luck, Mr Fowler?
FOWLER (*moving up* L *of the sofa*) I'm afraid not. I shall try again, of course. I'm quite sure there's been some mistake—a telegram wrongly addressed. or something.
MISS COOPER. I expect so.
FOWLER. I don't want anyone to wait up, but as I can hear the front-door bell from my room, I wonder if you'd mind if I answer it myself tonight?
MISS COOPER. That's quite all right, Mr Fowler, but you're surely not still expecting him, are you?
FOWLER (*crosing to the arch up* R) He might have hired a car, you know. He's a very extravagant boy. You know what these artists are. Well, good night.
MISS COOPER. Good night, Mr Fowler.

(FOWLER *exits up* R. MISS COOPER *rises, crosses and replaces the cushion in the chair* LC.

JOHN *enters up* R *and sits moodily in the easy chair above the fireplace.* MISS COOPER *moves to the pouffe, pours a cup of Mrs Railton-Bell's unwanted coffee and silently hands it to* JOHN, *who looks up at her, takes the coffee and sips it.* MISS COOPER *moves behind John's chair and affectionately kisses the top of his head*)

(*Gently*) Are you very drunk?
JOHN. No.
MISS COOPER. How many?
JOHN. As many as I could afford. It wasn't a lot.

(*There is a pause*)

MISS COOPER. Something's the matter, isn't it?
JOHN. Nothing much.
MISS COOPER. Want to tell me?
JOHN. I can't tell you.
MISS COOPER (*cheerfully*) That's all right. (*She sits on the fender*) What did you say to the old women?
JOHN. Too much. Far too damn much. Oh, God! (*He puts his

cup on the coffee table in front of the fire, rises and crosses above the sofa towards the window)

(Miss Cooper *anxiously watches him*)

I may have to leave.

Miss Cooper (*sharply*) You can't leave. (*She rises and moves above the armchair* RC)

John. I may have to.

Miss Cooper. You won't have to. I'll see to that. But was it so bad?

John (*over his shoulder; bitterly*) Not very bad, I suppose. Just an ordinary show-off, a rather sordid little piece of alcoholic self-assertion. (*He turns and moves to* R *of the sofa*) Taking it out on two old women, telling them what a brilliant political thinker I am, hinting at what a great man I once was. I even gave away that I used to work in the docks.

Miss Cooper. Oh, Lord!

John. And that I knew Roger Williamson. I think I covered that up, though. I hope I did.

Miss Cooper. I hope you did, too—(*she sits on the right side of the sofa*) otherwise old Railton-Bell will be on to it like a bloodhound.

John. I don't know. I can't think now. I'll remember it all in the morning. (*Miserably*) Oh, Pat. I'm so sorry. (*He stands* R *of her and puts his hand on her shoulder*)

Miss Cooper (*resting her cheek on his hand*) That's all right. I'll cover up for you. You'd better finish your coffee.

(John *moves obediently to the easy chair above the fire, sits and picks up his coffee*)

John. Why do I do these things? I used to know how to behave.

Miss Cooper (*turning to him*) I'd do them, too, in your place.

John. Don't over-dramatize me. I do that enough myself. I'd probably have been nothing, anyhow.

Miss Cooper. What about that newspaper cutting about yourself you showed me, which prophesied . . .

John. One political tipster napping an outsider. If nothing happens his tip is forgotten. If, by a fluke, it does, he can say: "Look how clever I was twenty years ago."

Miss Cooper. But before you were even thirty you'd been made a Junior Minister . . .

John (*brusquely*) Yes, yes, yes. It doesn't matter. The world is full of promising young men who haven't, in middle age, fulfilled their promise. There's nothing to that. Nothing at all. (*He puts his cup on the coffee table and stares at the floor*)

Miss Cooper (*quietly*) I wish you'd tell me what's happened.

John. I can't. I've told you I can't. But it's not important.

Miss Cooper. Important enough for quite a few whiskies.

JOHN. A lot of things are important enough for that. The day I heard Willy Barker had been made Minister of Economic Co-ordination, I had a bottle.

(*There is a pause, during which* MISS COOPER *rises, moves to* L *of John and puts her left hand on his shoulder*)

MISS COOPER. Couldn't you *ever* get back?

(JOHN *laughs sharply.* MISS COOPER *withdraws her hand*)

JOHN. God, what a field day for the Tory press that would be. John Malcolm Ramsden has decided to stand as a Labour Independent for his old constituency. It will be recalled that Mr Ramsden, who was Junior Minister in the nineteen forty-five administration, went to prison for six months in nineteen forty-six on the triple charge of assaulting a police officer in the course of his duty, of being drunk and disorderly, and of causing grievous bodily harm to his wife. The headline—"Gaol-Bird Stands Again". (*He rises and crosses down* C) No, thank you. I'll stay John Malcolm, journalist, middle-aged soak and has-been, the terror of the older lady residents of the *Hotel Beauregard*, Bournemouth. That's vastly preferable, I assure you. (*He sits on the sofa at the left side*)

(MISS COOPER, *before she speaks, sits in the armchair* RC)

MISS COOPER. John dear, I don't want to know what it is, but let me help you, if I can.

(JOHN *turns, gazes at her and puts his hand near her*)

JOHN (*simply*) Do you know, Pat, that I love you very sincerely?
MISS COOPER (*with a smile*) Sincerely? That sounds a little like what a brother says to a sister.
JOHN (*with an answering smile*) You have surely reason enough to know that my feelings for you can transcend the fraternal.

(MISS COOPER *rises and moves to* JOHN, *who puts his hand on her arm*)

MISS COOPER. Yes; but for all that—and don't think I'm not grateful for all that—not really quite enough reason. (*She puts her hand on his*)

(ANNE *enters up* R. JOHN *and* MISS COOPER *move apart, not in alarm, but as if from long practice.* MISS COOPER *picks up the coffee tray*)

(*She moves to the arch up* R. *Brightly*) Oh, hullo, Mrs Shankland. They told me you'd gone up some time ago.
ANNE. I had, but not to bed. I was reading.
MISS COOPER. That's a comfy armchair in there, isn't it?

Anne. Very. (*She stands, uncertainly, just inside the room looking at John*)

(John, *after a brief glance at Anne, turns slightly away from her*)

Miss Cooper. Was there anything you wanted, Mrs Shankland?

Anne (*diffidently*) No. I just wanted a word or two with Mr Malcolm.

Miss Cooper (*brightly again*) Oh, really? Had you two met before?

Anne. Yes. A long time ago.

Miss Cooper. Oh. (*She glances at John, evidently disturbed at the danger to his anonymity inherent in this situation, but she gets no answering look*) Oh, well. I'll leave you two alone, then. If you want anything, I shall be up for quite a time yet.

(Miss Cooper *exits up* R. Anne *gazes steadily at her ex-husband, but he is still looking away from her*)

Anne (*moving in*) I didn't want to go away without our saying something to each other, John. I hope you don't mind.

John. Mind? Why should I mind?

Anne. Your rushing out of dinner like a whirlwind made it look as if you hated the very sight of me.

(John *rises, turns slowly and looks fully at her for the first time*)

John. The very sight of you, Anne, is perhaps the one thing about you that I don't hate.

Anne (*with a slight nervous laugh*) Oh, dear! That's not very nice to hear.

John. Don't you enjoy being complimented on your looks any more? Has your narcissism vanished?

Anne. No, I suppose not. But I don't enjoy being hated by you.

John. Don't you? You used to.

Anne (*moving above the sofa; slowly*) You've got me wrong, John. You always did, you know.

John (*quietly*) I don't think so, Anne. If I had I wouldn't have found you so predictable.

Anne. You always used to say I was predictable. I remember that was one of the things that used to irritate me most. It's such an easy thing to say, and so impossible to disprove.

John. Yes, yes. Go to bed, Anne, and disappear quietly tomorrow. It's better, really it is. (*He sits on the head of the sofa, facing* L, *with his back to her*)

Anne. No, John. Let me stay just a little longer. (*She moves to the pouffe*) May I sit down?

John (*with a glance over his shoulder*) Is that a way of reminding me of my bad manners? I know I shouldn't sit while you're standing.

ANNE (*laughing gently*) You're so bristly. Even bristlier now than before. (*She sits on the pouffe, facing* R) Your manners were always very good.

JOHN (*turning away*) You used to tick me off about them often enough.

ANNE. Well—only sometimes—when we had silly conventional people at the flat who didn't understand you as I did.

JOHN (*with a faint smile*) I think if I'd been given time, I could have predicted that answer.

ANNE (*looking away* R; *with an answering smile*) Oh, dear! Tell me, did you always find me so predictable—even at the very beginning?

JOHN. Yes.

ANNE. Why did you marry me, then?

JOHN (*without looking at her*) If it pleases your vanity to hear my answer once again, you shall.

(ANNE *slowly looks round at him*)

Because my love for you at that time was so desperate, my craving for you was so violent, that I could refuse you nothing that you asked—not even a marriage that every prompting of reason told me must be disastrous.

ANNE. Why did it so necessarily have to be disastrous?

JOHN. Because of class, mainly.

ANNE. Class? Oh, that's nonsense, John. It's just inverted snobbery.

JOHN. No, I don't think so. The gulf between Kensington Gore and the Hull docks is still fairly wide. I was one of a family of eight, as I must have told you many times, and my views of a wife's duties must have been at least a little coloured by watching my mother sacrifice her health, strength and comfort, and eventually her life to looking after us children, and to keeping the old man out of trouble. I'm not saying my demands on a wife would have been pitched as high as that. But they would, I think, at least, have included the proper running of a home and the begetting of children.

ANNE (*hotly*) But, about children, I did make it perfectly clear before our marriage . . .

JOHN. Yes. You made it perfectly clear. A famous model mustn't gamble her figure merely for posterity. I accepted the bargain, Anne, the whole bargain. I have no complaint.

ANNE (*rising angrily*) You have, John, you know you have. (*She moves to the fireplace and looks in the mirror over the mantelpiece*) Your real complaint is still the same as it always was—that I didn't love you when we got married.

JOHN. Oh, God! Do we have to go into that again?

ANNE (*crossing above the sofa to the chair* LC) Yes, we do, it needs clearing up. You admitted just now that I was the one who wanted the marriage. All right. If that's true—which it is—what could have been the motive, except love? (*She sits on the chair* LC *and puts her bag on the seat beside her*) Oh, yes. I know. You were a Junior Minister at the time, but let's face it, there were even grander figures that I might have . . .

JOHN (*interrupting*) I know, Anne dear. I remember it all in detail. A duke, a baronet, an Australian millionaire, and that film producer.

ANNE. Well, then?

JOHN (*quietly*) You married me because you were frightened. You were going to be thirty. You'd realized suddenly that you couldn't go on for the rest of your life gazing joyously at yourself in the mirror, because the time would come when what you saw in the mirror would no longer give you joy. And you couldn't go on treading happily on the faces of all the men who wanted you, because the time would come when there wouldn't be so many faces to tread on.

ANNE. Eloquent John, but unconvincing. If so, why not a baronet's or a millionaire's wife? Why Mrs Ramsden?

JOHN. Because the others couldn't pay you the full price.

ANNE. What price?

JOHN. The price you put on yourself when you so reluctantly settled for giving yourself to the highest bidder in marriage.

ANNE. You mean a title wasn't enough?

JOHN. No.

ANNE. Nor a million?

JOHN Nor a million.

ANNE. What was the price, then?

JOHN. Enslavement.

ANNE. John, really. How ridiculous you are. I seem to remember this accusation from the old days.

JOHN. I've no doubt you do.

ANNE. If all I wanted to do was to make my husband a slave, why should I specially have chosen you and not the others?

JOHN. Because where would your fun have been in enslaving the sort of man who was already the slave of his own head gardener? (*He rises and crosses to the fireplace*) You wanted bigger game. Wilder game. None of your baronets and Australian millionaires, too well-mannered to protest when you denied them their conjugal rights, and too well-brought-up not to take your headaches at bedtime as just headaches at bedtime. (*Over his shoulder*) "Poor old girl! Bad show! So sorry. Better in the morning, I hope. Feeling a bit tired myself, anyway." (*He turns to face her*) No, Anne dear. What enjoyment would there have been for you in using your weapons on that sort of a husband? But to turn them on a genuine, live, roaring savage from the slums of Hull, to make him grovel at the vague and distant promise of delights that were his anyway by right, or goad him to such a frenzy of drink and rage by a locked door that he'd kick it in and hit you with his fist so hard that you'd knock yourself unconscious against a wall—that must really have been fun.

(*There is a long pause.* ANNE's *face is without expression as she looks at him*)

ANNE (*at length*) Goodness, John, how you do go on.

JOHN. Yes. I do. You must forgive me. It's a foible, perhaps, of disappointed politicians. Besides, tonight I'm rather drunker than usual. (*He turns away to the fireplace*)

ANNE (*with a hint of eagerness*) Because of seeing me? (*She rises, moves to* L *of the sofa and puts her stole on it*)

JOHN (*turning to face her*) Yes.

ANNE. I'm sorry.

JOHN. No, you're not. (*He turns away*)

(ANNE *laughs, quite gaily now, and with far more confidence. She sits on the sofa, puts her feet up and lies back*)

ANNE. You haven't changed much, have you?

JOHN. Haven't I?

ANNE. The same old John pouring out the same old cascade of of truths, half-truths and distortions, all beaten up together to make a neat, consistent story. *Your* story. Human nature isn't quite as simple as you make it, John. You've left out the most important fact of all.

JOHN. What's that?

ANNE. That you're the only person in the world I've ever been really fond of. You notice how tactfully I leave out the word love. Give me a cigarette.

(JOHN *crosses to* R *of the sofa, takes a packet of cigarettes from his pocket and offers it to Anne*)

Oh, not *still* those awful cork-tipped things. (*A faint note of authority creeps back into her voice*) I'll have one of my own. Hand me my bag.

(JOHN *moves obediently round the top of the sofa, picks up Anne's bag from the chair* LC, *hands it to her, then sits on the desk chair. There is a pause, as* ANNE *takes a gold cigarette case from her bag, and lights a cigarette.* JOHN, *not looking at her, plays with a piece of crumpled paper*)

Well—do you dispute that?

JOHN (*without looking at her*) I might observe that your fondness for me was sometimes shown in rather surprising ways.

ANNE. Well, I wasn't prepared to be your doormat. I had to fight back sometimes, didn't I?

John. I suppose so. It was your choice of weapons that was unfair. (*He looks at her*)

Anne. I didn't have any others. You had the brains and the eloquence and the ability to make me feel cheap—which incidentally you've done again tonight.

John (*looking down*) Have I? I'm sorry. (*He throws the piece of paper into the waste-paper basket*)

Anne. Anyway, isn't it a principle of war that you always play on the opponent's weakness?

John. A principle of war, not necessarily of marriage.

Anne. Marriage is a kind of war.

John. It is for you.

Anne (*with a smile*) For you, too, John. Be fair now.

John (*after a pause; looking at her over the back of the chair*) And the weakness you played on was my overpowering love for you?

Anne. You can put it that way if you like. There are less pretty-sounding ways.

(John *remains silent, looking at* Anne *as she smokes her cigarette, through a holder, now plainly quite confident of herself*)

Besides, you and I never could have agreed on *that* aspect of married life.

John. No. We couldn't.

Anne. Why are you staring at me?

John. You know very well why.

Anne (*contentedly*) Well, don't. It makes me embarrassed.

John. I'm sorry. (*He turns away*)

Anne. You really think I haven't changed much—to look at, I mean?

John (*without looking at her*) Not at all.

Anne. Just a clever make-up, I expect.

John. I don't think so.

Anne. John, if you'd wanted an obedient little *hausfrau* for a wife, why didn't you marry one—like that manageress I caught you canoodling with a moment ago? That *was* a canoodle, wasn't it?

John. A canoodle is what you would call it, yes.

Anne. Why haven't you married her?

John. Because I'm not in love with her.

Anne. Does that matter?

John. I'm old-fashioned enough to think it does.

Anne. Couldn't you—as they say—*learn* to love her? After all, she's your type.

John. I have still only one type in the world, Anne. God knows it does little for my pride to have to admit that to you, but I never was very good at lying about myself. (*He rises, takes a step towards her and looks at her*) Only one type. The prototype.

ANNE (*looking at him; quietly*) I'm glad.

JOHN. I've no doubt you are. Tell me, does a compliment still give you that little jab in the solar plexus that you used to describe to me?

ANNE. Yes, it does. More so than ever now that I'm forty. There —I've admitted it.

JOHN (*moving to* L *of the sofa*) I'd worked it out anyway.

(*They both laugh quietly*)

(*He picks up her cigarette case*) That's a nice little affair. Who gave you that? Your second?

ANNE. Yes.

JOHN. He had good taste.

ANNE. In jewels.

JOHN (*returning the case to her*) You ought to have made a go of it with that man. He sounds much more your form.

ANNE. He wasn't a man. He was a mouse. (*She puts her feet down and sits on the right side of the sofa*)

JOHN. Didn't he pay you enough compliments?

ANNE. Too many, and none of them meant.

JOHN. No solar plexus? (*He turns away upstage*)

ANNE. No. John——

(JOHN *comes back behind her*)

(*She touches his sleeve suddenly in an intimate, friendly gesture*) —I'm in a bad way, you know.

JOHN. I'm sorry.

ANNE. Some of the things you used to tell me might happen to me *are* happening.

JOHN. Such as?

ANNE. Loneliness—for one. (*She withdraws her hand*)

JOHN. No friends?

ANNE. Not many. I haven't the gift.

JOHN. There's no gift. To make people love you is a gift, and you have it.

ANNE (*bitterly*) Had it.

JOHN. Have it.

ANNE. And yet I hate being alone. Oh God, how I hate it. This place, for instance, gives me the creeps.

JOHN (*innocently*) Why did you come here, then?

(ANNE, *for the briefest instant, looks startled, but recovers at at once*)

ANNE. I suppose I didn't realize what it would be like. Oh, God! What a life. I can just see myself in a few years' time at one of those separate tables . . .

JOHN. Is there no-one on the horizon?

Anne. No-one that I'd want. And time is slipping. God, it goes fast, doesn't it?

John. I haven't found it so, these last eight years.

Anne (*turning to him*) Poor John, I'm so sorry. (*She takes his hand*) But it's such a wonderful fluke our meeting again like this, that we really shouldn't waste it. We must see some more of each other now. After all when fate plays as astounding a trick as this on us, it must mean something, mustn't it? Don't send me away tomorrow. Let me stay on a little while. (*She lies back on the sofa*)

(John *makes no reply. He is staring at her*)

(*Gently*) I won't be a nuisance.

(John *still does not answer. He is still staring at her*)

I won't, John. Really I won't.

John (*at length; murmuring thickly*) You won't be a nuisance? (*He embraces her suddenly and violently*)

(Anne *responds. After a moment she begins to say something*)

(*Savagely*) Don't speak. For God's sake don't speak. You'll kill this moment.

(Anne *rises, moves to the fireplace, stubs her cigarette out in the ashtray on the coffee table, then stands* L *of the easy chair above the fireplace*)

Anne. John, darling John, even at the risk of "killing your moment" I think I really *must* say something. I think I must remind you that we are in a public lounge, and inform you that Miss Cooper has been good enough to give me what appears to be a very isolated room, the number of which is—(*she picks up her handbag, extracts a key and looks at the number*) nineteen. Give me one of those horrid cork-tipped things of yours. I'm right out of mine. (*She moves to* R *of the sofa, picks up her stole and puts it on*)

(John *takes his cigarettes from his pocket and brusquely thrusts the packet at her.* Anne *takes a cigarette.* John *tenders his lighter. His hand is trembling*)

Oh—what a shaky hand. (*She holds John's hand still and lights her cigarette*)

(John *thrusts his hand back into his coat pocket and keeps it there*)

(*She moves to the fireplace, smooths her dress, makes some adjustment to her hair and turns to him*) How do I look? All right?

John (*murmuring*) All right. Half an hour

Anne (*happily blowing him a kiss*) Darling John.

John (*not returning the gesture*) Darling Anne.

ANNE (*moving up* R *of the sofa and collecting her bag*) Half an hour?

MISS COOPER (*off*) Mrs Shankland . . .

ANNE (*smiling at John*) You see?

(MISS COOPER *enters up* R)

MISS COOPER. Oh, Mrs Shankland—you're wanted on the tele-phone—a London call.

ANNE. Oh? Where is the telephone?

MISS COOPER. I'll show you. It's just through there.

(ANNE *and* MISS COOPER *exit up* R. JOHN, *left alone, sits down suddenly on the left side of the sofa, as if his knees had weakened. He rests his head on his hands.*

MISS COOPER *enters up* R. *She stands above the armchair* RC *and looks at John for a moment before she speaks*)

That's her, isn't it?

JOHN. What?

MISS COOPER. Mrs Shankland. That's the one, isn't it?

JOHN. Yes.

MISS COOPER. She looks exactly the way you described her. Carved in ice, you said once, I remember.

JOHN. Did I?

MISS COOPER. What's going to happen now, John?

(JOHN *looks up at her without replying. There is a pause*)

(*She moves to* L *of the sofa. Quietly*) I see. Well, I always knew you were still in love with her and always would be. You never made any bones about that.

JOHN (*turning to her; pleadingly*) Pat, dearest . . .

MISS COOPER. No. You don't need to say anything. I under-stand. So you'll be going away, will you?

JOHN. I don't know. Oh, God! I don't know.

MISS COOPER (*moving to the french windows*) I expect you will. She looks as if she's got some will-power, that girl. If she's taken that much trouble to run you to earth down here, she won't let you go so easily. (*She adjusts the curtains*)

JOHN. She hasn't run me to earth. It was a coincidence her coming down here.

MISS COOPER (*turning to him*) Coincidence? Do you really believe that?

JOHN. Yes.

MISS COOPER. All right, then. I'm not saying anything. (*She crosses towards the arch up* R)

JOHN (*rising and intercepting her*) Say it.

MISS COOPER (*continuing to the arch up* R) No, I won't.

(JOHN *grabs her fiercely by the arms and turns her round*)

John (*fiercely*) Say it. Say it, damn you.

Miss Cooper (*quietly*) Don't knock me about, John. I'm not her, you know.

(John *relaxes his grip*)

All right. I'll say it. If it was coincidence, why is she talking to the editor of the *New Outlook* on the telephone now?

John. What?

Miss Cooper. His name's Wilder, isn't it?

John. Yes.

Miss Cooper. Terminus number?

John. Yes.

Miss Cooper. And he knows who you really are, doesn't he, and where you live?

John. Yes.

Miss Cooper. And he goes around the West End quite a bit, I'd imagine—cocktail parties and things?

(John *turns his back to her and leans on the back of the desk chair*)

Mind you, it could be a different Mr Wilder, I suppose. If there's one coincidence—why not another?

(Anne *enters up* R. *She looks happy and unruffled*)

Anne (*to Miss Cooper*) Thank you so much, Miss Cooper. I'm going to bed now. I've put down a call for eight-thirty with hot water and lemon. I hope that's all right?

Miss Cooper. Quite all right, Mrs Shankland.

Anne. Well, good night. Good night, Mr Malcolm.

John. Stay here, Anne. Pat, you go.

Miss Cooper (*moving to John; urgently*) Not now, John. Leave it till the morning.

(Anne *moves above the armchair* RC)

John. It's got to be now. Leave us alone, Pat, please.

(Miss Cooper *exits quietly up* R)

(*He moves to the sofa*) When fate plays as astounding a trick as this it must mean something, Anne, mustn't it?

Anne. Yes. that's what I said.

John (*harshly*) What did you tell Wilder?

(Anne *opens her mouth to speak*)

(*He takes a step or two towards her*) No, no. There's no need to lie any more. I'll quote you, shall I? My dear, our little plot's gone off quite wonderfully. Thank you so much for your help. Ten minutes alone with him was all I needed to have him grovelling. My dear, it was too funny, but after only one kiss his hand was shaking so much he couldn't even light my cigarette. You should have seen it. You'd have died laughing. Oh, yes. He's at my feet again all right, and I can tread on his face just any time I like from now on.

(JOHN *advances slowly and stands facing* ANNE, *who stands her ground, looks a little scared, then sits on the left arm of the easy chair above the fireplace*)

ANNE (*sincerely*) John, please don't be so angry with me. It's not as if I'd done anything so terrible. I had to see you again. I was desperate to see you again, and this was the only way I could think of.

JOHN. The only way *you* could think of, of course. You wouldn't have thought of writing me a letter, or ringing me up—(*he points to the dining-room door*) or telling me the truth in there? Oh, no. You had to have your conquest, you had to have your unconditional surrender, and if you could do it by lying and cheating, so much the better. It makes the greater triumph.

ANNE. That's not true. Really it isn't. Oh, yes I should have told you, John. Of course I should have told you, but you see even now I've still got a little pride left.

JOHN. And so have I, Anne, thank God. So have I. (*He puts his hands on her arms and pulls her close to him, staring at her face*) Yes, I can see the make-up now all right. Yes, Anne, I can see little lines there that weren't there before. (*He slips his hand on to her throat*) There'll soon be nothing left to drive a man to . . .

ANNE (*quietly*) Why don't you? Why don't you?

(JOHN *stands looking down at her for a moment, then suddenly throws her to the floor in front of the fireplace. The coffee table is overturned.* JOHN *goes to the french windows, pulls them open and runs out. The wind blows the curtains into the room.* ANNE *lies quite still for a few moments, her face expressionless, then she gets up, sobbing, turns to the fireplace and stares at herself for a long time in the mirror over the mantelpiece. She turns quickly away, sobs quietly at first, and then more violently, until, as she makes her way blindly to the arch up* R, *it is uncontrollable.*

MISS COOPER *enters up* R, *before* ANNE *has reached the arch.* ANNE, *seeing her, barring the way, runs back and sits on the desk chair, still sobbing.* MISS COOPER *crosses and deliberately closes the french windows before turning to Anne. Then she stands* R *of Anne, and puts a hand on her shoulder*)

MISS COOPER. Come to my room, won't you, Mrs Shankland? There's a fire there and a nice comfortable chair, and I've even got a little sherry, I think. We'll be quite cosy there and no-one can disturb us.

(ANNE *rises*)

(*She begins to move Anne towards the arch up* R) You see, someone might come in here, and we don't want that, do we? Come
along now, Mrs Shankland. Come along.

    MISS COOPER *is leading* ANNE *towards the arch up* R *as the
lights dim and*—

the CURTAIN *falls*

SCENE III

SCENE—*The dining-room. The following morning.*

When the CURTAIN *rises,* MISS MEACHAM *is at her table, eating her breakfast and poring over the sporting page of a morning paper.* CHARLES *and* JEAN *are seated at their table, finishing their breakfast, and reading.* MRS RAILTON-BELL *and* LADY MATHESON *have already finished their breakfast.* ANNE *and* JOHN's *tables are vacant. They have not yet had breakfast.* FOWLER *has had his breakfast and his table is unoccupied.*

MISS COOPER (*off in the lounge*) Yes, Mrs Railton-Bell, I promise I will.

(MISS COOPER *appears in the doorway up* LC)

(*Over her shoulder*) Yes, utterly disgraceful, I quite agree. I shall speak to him most severely. (*She closes the door with a faint sigh. To Charles and Jean. Brightly*) Good morning, Miss Tanner. Good morning, Mr Stratton.

(CHARLES *and* JEAN *reply with a polite murmur and plunge back into their books*)

(*She moves to* L *of Miss Meacham's table*) Good morning, Miss Meacham. It looks as if we're going to have a nice dry day at last.

MISS MEACHAM. Is it going to be dry at Newbury? That's the point. "Walled Garden's" a dog on heavy going.

MISS COOPER. Ah, now there you have me, Miss Meacham.

(MABEL *enters from the kitchen and crosses to* L *of Mrs Railton-Bell's table.* MISS COOPER *picks up the napkins from Mrs Railton-Bell's and Lady Matheson's tables and puts them in the alcove*)

MABEL. Miss Cooper, Mr Malcolm wasn't in his room when I took his tea up, and his bed hadn't been slept in.

MISS COOPER (*with a reassuring smile*) Yes, I know, Mabel.

MABEL. You know?

MISS COOPER (*turning and pushing the chair into Lady Matheson's table*) I should have told you, of course, but I'm afraid I clean forgot. He had to go to London unexpectedly last night.

MABEL. He won't be in to breakfast, then?

MISS COOPER (*moving to Mrs Railton-Bell's table*) I don't suppose so.

(CHARLES *and* JEAN *rise and exit up* LC)

MABEL. That's something, anyway. It's nearly ten now. What about the new lady? She's not down yet.

MISS COOPER. Yes, she's down, Mabel, but I don't think she's having breakfast.

MABEL. Not having breakfast?

MISS COOPER. She has to be very careful of her figure, you see.

MABEL (*with puzzled gloom*) Can't see what good a figure's going to be to you, when you're dead of starvation.

(MABEL *exits to the kitchen*)

MISS MEACHAM. She's leaving, isn't she, the new one?

MISS COOPER (*moving* C) Yes. She is. How did you know?

MISS MEACHAM. I heard her ask for her bags to be brought down. I knew she'd never stick it.

MISS COOPER (*coldly*) *Stick* it, Miss Meacham?

MISS MEACHAM. Oh, I don't mean the hotel. Best for the price in Bournemouth. I've always said so. I meant the life. All this. (*She indicates the empty tables*) She's not an "alone" type.

MISS COOPER. Is any type an "alone" type, Miss Meacham?

MISS MEACHAM. Oh, yes. They're rare, of course, but *you* are, for one, I'd say.

MISS COOPER. Am I?

MISS MEACHAM (*pouring a cup of tea for herself*) Oh, I'm not saying you won't fall in love one day, and get married, or something silly like that. I'm only saying that if you don't, you'll be all right. You're self-sufficient.

MISS COOPER (*collecting the napkins from the table up* C; *a shade wearily, but polite*) I'm glad you think so. Miss Meacham. Perhaps even a little gladder than you realize.

MISS MEACHAM. What do you mean by that?

MISS COOPER. I've no idea. I'm a bit tired this morning. I had very little sleep last night. (*She stands a little down stage of the table up* C)

MISS MEACHAM. Well—I don't suppose you *are* glad, really. Probably you haven't had to face up to it yet. I faced up to it very early on—long before I was an old wreck—while I was still young and pretty and had money and position and could choose from quite a few. (*Reminiscently*) Quite a few.

(MISS COOPER *puts the napkins in the alcove then stands by Mrs Railton-Bell's table*)

Well, I didn't choose any of them, and I've never regretted it—not for an instant. People have always scared me a bit, you see. They're so complicated. I suppose that's why I prefer the dead ones. Any trouble from them and you switch them off like a television set. (*She rises*) No, what I've always said is—being alone. that's the real blessed state—if you've the character for it. Not Mrs What's-her-name from Mayfair, though. I could tell that at a glance. A couple of week's here and she'd have her head in the gas oven. It's pork for lunch, isn't it?

MISS COOPER. Yes, Miss Meacham.

MISS MEACHAM. I loathe pork. Ah, well, I'd have a bit on "Walled Garden", dear, if I were you. He's past the post if the going's on top.

(MISS MEACHAM *exits up* LC. MISS COOPER, *left alone, slumps wearily into the chair Miss Meacham has vacated. She lets her head fall forward on to her chest, in an attitude of utter exhaustion. There is a slight pause.*

JOHN *enters slowly up* LC)

JOHN (*in a low voice*) Pat. I must see you a moment.

(MISS COOPER *opens her eyes and looks up at John. She jumps to her feet as she takes him in*)

MISS COOPER. Are you all right?

JOHN. Yes, I'm all right.

MISS COOPER. Where did you go?

JOHN. I don't know. I walked a long way.

MISS COOPER. Were you out all night?

JOHN. No. I sat in a shelter for a time. Pat, I've got to have some money. I'm broke to the wide. I spent my whole week's cheque in the *Feathers* last night.

MISS COOPER. How much do you want?

JOHN. Enough to get me on a train and keep me some place for a few days. Three or four pounds, I suppose. Can you let me have it, Pat?

MISS COOPER. You won't need it, John. She's going.

JOHN. Are you sure?

MISS COOPER. Yes.

JOHN. Where is she now?

MISS COOPER. In my office. It's all right. She won't come in here. (*She feels his clothes*) Did you get very wet? (*She feels his hands*)

JOHN. Yes, I suppose so. It's dried off now.

MISS COOPER (*crossing below John to his table and pulling out the chair*) You'd better sit down and have some breakfast. Your hands are like ice.

JOHN (*crossing to his table*) I don't want anything to eat. Just some tea.

MISS COOPER (*standing* L *of John's table*) All right. Now sit down. Straighten your tie a bit and turn your collar down.

(JOHN *tidies himself*)

That's better. Now you look quite respectable.

(JOHN *sits at his table*)

Doreen *enters from the kitchen and crosses to* L *of the table* C)

Doreen (*seeing John*) Oh, you back? I suppose you think you can have breakfast at this time?

Miss Cooper. Just some tea, Doreen—that's all.

Doreen. Oh, okey-doke.

(Doreen *exits to the kitchen*)

Miss Cooper. She'll have to go, that girl. (*She turns to John*) Well, that was a fine way to behave, dashing out into the night, and scaring us out of our wits.

John. Us?

Miss Cooper. Oh, yes. She was scared, too. I stopped her from calling the police.

John. So you talked to her, did you?

Miss Cooper. Most of the night. She was a bit hysterical and needed quieting. I didn't want to get a doctor.

John. Pat, tell me the truth—did I hurt her?

Miss Cooper. Her throat? No.

John. She fell, though, didn't she? I seem to remember pushing her, and her falling and hitting her head—or perhaps I'm confusing it with . . .

Miss Cooper (*firmly*) She's as right as rain. There isn't a mark on her of any kind.

John (*murmuring*) Thank God!

(Miss Cooper *turns away up stage.*

Doreen *enters from the kitchen. She carries a tray with a pot of tea and a plate of biscuits.* John *takes a cigarette from his case, and lights it*)

Doreen (*crossing and serving John*) I brought you some digestive biscuits. I know you like them.

John. Thank you. Thank you, Doreen, very much.

Doreen. Oh, have you had a tumble or something? You've got mud all over your arm.

(Miss Cooper *turns*)

John. What? Oh, yes. So I have. Yes, I remember now. I fell down last night in the dark.

Doreen. Oh, well— give it to me after and I'll get it off.

(Doreen *crosses and exits to the kitchen*)

Miss Cooper. I should have seen that. I'm sorry.

John. It's all right. They'll just think I was drunk. How is she this morning?

Miss Cooper. A bit shaky. Quieter, though. (*She gets a chair from* R *of the table up* C *and puts it* L *of John's table*) Did you know she took drugs?

JOHN. Drugs? What sort of drugs?

MISS COOPER. Oh, just those things that make you sleep. Only she takes about three times the proper dose and takes them in the day, too.

JOHN. How long has this been going on?

MISS COOPER. About a year, I gather.

JOHN. The damn little fool! Why does she do it?

MISS COOPER (*shrugging*) Why do you go to the *Feathers*?

(*There is a pause*)

Yes—there's not all that much to choose between you, I'd say. When you're together you slash each other to pieces, and when you're apart you slash yourselves to pieces. All told, it's quite a problem. (*She pours a cup of tea for John*)

(*There is a pause*)

JOHN. Why didn't she tell me about this last night?

MISS COOPER. Because she's what she is, that's why. If she'd shown you she was unhappy, she'd have had to show you how much she needed you, and that she'd never do—not her—not in a million years. Of course that's why she lied about coming down here. (*She hands John the cup of tea then sits* L *of his table*) I've got rather a bad conscience about that, you know. I should never have told you. Just a flash of jealousy, I suppose. I'm sorry.

JOHN. What time is she leaving. (*He drinks his tea*)

MISS COOPER. She's only waiting now to get some news of you. I was just going to start ringing up the hospitals. She asked me to do that.

JOHN. I see. (*He drinks*) Well, when I've finished this I'll slip out somewhere. Then when she's gone you can give me a ring. You can tell her that I'm quite all right.

MISS COOPER. You don't think you might tell her that yourself?

(*There is a pause*)

JOHN. No. (*He puts down his cup*)

MISS COOPER. It's your business, of course, but I think if I were in your place I'd want to.

JOHN (*savagely*) You don't know what it's like to be in my place. You can't even guess.

MISS COOPER (*rising and replacing her chair; quietly*) I think I can. Gosh, I'm tired. I shouldn't be sitting here gossiping with you. I've got work to do. You'd better let me tell her you're here. (*She stands* R *of the table up* C)

JOHN. No, Pat. Don't. Give me one reason why I should ever see her again. Just one.

MISS COOPER. All right. (*With a step towards him*) Just one, then. And God knows it's not for me to say it. Because you love her and because she needs your help.

(*There is a pause*)

John (*suspiciously*) What went on between you two last night?
How did she win you over?

Miss Cooper (*with a step away*) She didn't win me over, for
heaven's sake! Feeling the way I do, do you think she could? Anyway, to do her justice, she didn't even try. (*She sits* R *of the table
up* C) She didn't give me an act, and I could see her as she is, all
right. I think all you've ever told me about her is probably true.
She *is* vain and spoiled and selfish and deceitful. Of course, with
you being in love with her, you look at all those faults like in a
kind of distorting mirror, so that they seem like monstrous sins
and drive you to—well—the sort of thing that happened last
night. Well. I just see them as ordinary human faults, that's all—
the sort of faults a lot of people have—mostly women, I grant, but
some men, too. I don't like them, but they don't stop me feeling
sorry for a woman who's unhappy and desperate and ill and
needing help more than anyone I have ever known. (*She rises*)
Well? Shall I call her in?

John. Don't interfere in this, Pat. Just let her go back to London
and her own life, and leave me to live the rest of mine in peace.

Miss Cooper (*quietly*) That'd be fine, John, if you'd just tell
me a little something first. Exactly what kind of peace *are* you
living in down here?

John. A kind of peace anyway.

Miss Cooper (*moving to* L *of him and putting a hand on his
shoulder*) Is it? Is it even really living?

    (John *makes no reply*)

Is it, John? Be honest, now. Oh, I know there's your work and
your pals at the *Feathers,* and—well—me—but is it even living?

    (*There is a pause*)

John (*at length; shortly*) It'll do.

Miss Cooper (*with a faint laugh*) Thank you. (*She turns away
from him*) I'm glad you didn't hand me one of those tactful tarra-
diddles. I *did* try—you know—when we first began—you and I—
all that time ago—I *did* try to help you to get back into some sort
of life. As a matter of fact I tried very hard.

John. I know you did.

Miss Cooper. It didn't take me long, though, to see I hadn't a
hope.

John. Don't blame me for that, Pat. Circumstances, as they say,
outside my control . . .

Miss Cooper (*turning to face him*) Outside your control? Yes.
That's right. (*Quite brightly*) When you think of it, it seems
really rather a pity you two ever met, doesn't it?

John. Yes. A great pity.

MISS COOPER (*brightly*) If you hadn't, she'd have been a millionairess and you'd have been Prime Minister and I'd have married Mr Hopkins from the bank, and then we'd all have been happy. (*She moves to the door up* LC) I'm going into the office now, and I'm going to tell her you're here. I've got to have a word with Mr Fowler first, about a room he didn't take up, so if you want to skedaddle, you can. There's the door and the street's outside, and down the street is the *Feathers*. It's a bit early, but I've no doubt they'll open for you.

(MISS COOPER *exits up* LC, *closing the door behind her.* JOHN, *left alone, rises and stands in evident doubt and irresolution. After a moment he moves towards the door up* LC.
DOREEN *enters from the kitchen*)

DOREEN. Have you finished?
JOHN. Not quite, Doreen.
DOREEN. Well—make up your mind. (*She begins to clear some things from Miss Meacham's table*)

(JOHN *goes to his table and sits. There is a pause.*
ANNE *enters up* LC. JOHN *does not look at her*)

Oh, hullo, Mrs Shankland. You're a bit late for breakfast, I'm afraid. I expect you didn't know. There's some coffee left, though, or tea if you'd rather, and I can get you some biscuits. Is that all right?
ANNE. Thank you. That's very kind. Coffee, please. Not tea.
DOREEN. Righty-oh!

(DOREEN *exits to the kitchen.* ANNE *stands up* LC)

ANNE (*pleadingly*) John . . .

(JOHN *does not look up*)

(*With a step towards him*) John . . .
JOHN (*quietly*) You'd better sit at your own table. She'll be back in a moment.
ANNE. Yes. Yes, I will. (*She moves to her table and sits*) I was desperately worried about you.
JOHN. You needn't have been. I was quite all right. How are *you* now?
ANNE. All right, too. (*After a pause*) I'm going this morning, you know.
JOHN. So I heard.
ANNE. I won't bother you again. Ever again. I just wanted to say I'm sorry I had to lie to you.
JOHN. Thank you, Anne.
ANNE. I don't know why I did. Not for the reasons you gave, I think, though they may be right, too, I admit. I don't seem to know very much about myself any more. I'm sorry. John.

JOHN. That's all right.

ANNE. I *am* an awful liar. I always have been—ever since school. I don't know why, but I'd rather lie than tell the truth even about the simplest things. (*With a wan smile*) It was nearly always about my lying that we used to quarrel in the old days—do you remember?

JOHN. Yes. I remember.

(ANNE *lowers her head quickly as the tears come suddenly*)

ANNE. Oh, John—I don't know what's going to happen to me . . .

(DOREEN *enters from the kitchen. She carries a tray with two plates of biscuits.* ANNE *turns her head quickly away from* DOREEN, *who crosses to John's table and puts down a plate of biscuits.* ANNE *manages to wipe her eyes unseen*)

DOREEN (*to John*) Thought you might like some more. I know your appetite. (*She puts the other plate of biscuits on Anne's table*) here you are, Mrs Shankland. Coffee's just coming.

(DOREEN, *having noticed nothing, exits to the kitchen*)

ANNE (*smiling again*) Narrow escape. I'm sorry. I'm in a rather weak state this morning.

JOHN. How much money exactly does Shankland give you, Anne?

ANNE. I've told you—fifty. (*She meets his eyes. At length, murmuring shamefacedly*) Fifteen hundred.

JOHN. Can't you live quite happily on that?

ANNE. How can *I* live happily on anything now?

JOHN. But you don't need to be alone in London. You may not have many friends, but you have hundreds of acquaintances, and surely you can go out and enjoy yourself.

ANNE. You can be more alone in London than in this place, John. Here at least you can talk from table to table. In London it's the phone and usually no answer.

(*There is a pause*)

JOHN. You must give up those drugs, Anne.

ANNE. She told you?

JOHN. They won't help, you know.

ANNE. I know they won't.

JOHN. Throw them all into the dustbin. They're no good, those things.

ANNE. I won't do that. I can't. I'm not strong enough. But I'll cut them down if I can.

JOHN. Try.

ANNE (*looking at him*) I *will* try. I promise.

(*There is a pause*)

JOHN. Tell me, Anne. When you say you need me, is it me you really mean, or just my love? Because if it's my love you must know now that you have that. You have that for life.

ANNE. It's you, John.

JOHN. But why? Why, for heaven's sake?

ANNE. I suppose because you're all the things I'm not. You're honest and true and sincere and dependable and—(*she breaks off and tries to smile*) Oh dear, this is just becoming a boring catalogue of your virtues. Too embarrassing. I'm sorry, and that damn waitress will come in and catch me crying again.

JOHN. I may have had some of those virtues once, Anne. I'm not at all sure that I have them now. So I don't know if I'd be able to satisfy your need. I do know, though, that you can never satisfy mine.

ANNE (*looking at him*) how can you know?

JOHN. Experience.

ANNE (*facing front*) Supposing I'd learnt something from the last eight years?

JOHN. It's not a lesson that can be taught.

ANNE. I could still try.

JOHN. So could I, Anne. So could I. And we'd both fail.

ANNE. How can you be so sure?

JOHN. Because our two needs for each other are like two chemicals that are harmless by themselves, but when brought together in a test-tube can make an explosive as deadly as dynamite.

ANNE (*looking down*) I could take the risk. After all, there are worse deaths, aren't there? (*She looks round the room at the empty tables*) Slower and more frightening. So frightening, John. So frightening. (*She lowers her head as once more the tears come*) I'm an awful coward, you see. I never have been able to face anything alone—the blitzes in the war, being ill, having operations, all that. And now I can't even face—just getting old.

(JOHN *rises quietly, moves the chair from Mrs Railton-Bell's table, sets it* R *of Anne's table and sits.* ANNE *has her head lowered and a handkerchief to her eyes, so that it is only when she has recovered herself a little that she finds him sitting there. She looks at him without saying anything.* JOHN *puts his hand on the table*)

JOHN (*gently*) You realize, don't you, that we haven't very much hope together?

(ANNE *nods, and holds his hand tight in hers*)

ANNE. Have we all that much apart?

(DOREEN *enters from the kitchen. She carries a tray with a pot of coffee and a cup and saucer. She crosses towards John's table, realizes he is not there, turns and sees him at Anne's table.* John *and* Anne *release their hands*)

Doreen. Oh. Do you want your tea over there?
John. Yes, please.

(Doreen *transfers John's cup to Anne's table, then serves Anne with the coffee*)

Thank you.
Doreen (*standing between them*) Do you two want to sit at the same table from now on? You can, if you like.
John. Yes. I think we do.
Doreen (*moving upstage*) Oh. I'll make up a double for you for lunch, then. It's just so long as we know.

Doreen *exits to the kitchen.* John *takes Anne's hand as—*

the Curtain *falls*

TABLE NUMBER SEVEN
A Play in Two Scenes

It is the author's wish that in all future productions
Table by the Window and *Table Number Seven* should
be known as *Table No. 1* and *Table No. 2* respectively.

TABLE NUMBER SEVEN

Produced at the St James's Theatre, London, on the 22nd September, 1954, with the following cast of characters:

(in the order of speaking)

MRS STRATTON	*Patricia Raine*
MR STRATTON	*Basil Henson*
MAJOR POLLOCK	*Eric Portman*
MR FOWLER	*Aubrey Mather*
MISS COOPER	*Beryl Measor*
MRS RAILTON-BELL	*Phyllis Neilson-Terry*
MISS RAILTON -BELL	*Margaret Leighton*
LADY MATHESON	*Jane Eccles*
MISS MEACHAM	*May Hallat*
MABEL	*Marion Fawcett*
DOREEN	*Priscilla Morgan*

Directed by PETER GLENVILLE
Settings by MICHAEL WEIGHT

SYNOPSIS OF SCENES

The action of the Play takes place at the Beauregard Private Hotel, Bournemouth, during the summer. Eighteen months later

SCENE I
The lounge. After tea

SCENE II
The dining-room. Dinner time

Time— the present

SCENE I

SCENE—*The lounge. After tea.*

It is eighteen months or so since the events of the preceding play.

When the CURTAIN *rises, it is a fine, summer afternoon and the french windows are open.* CHARLES STRATTON, *in flannels and sports shirt, sits astride on the sofa, reading a large medical treatise.* MRS STRATTON *née* JEAN TANNER, *enters by the french windows, pushing a small pram.*

JEAN (*to the unseen baby*) Tum along now. Tum along. (*She stands the pram* L *of the sofa*) Tum and see daddy—daddy will give you a little tiss and then beddy-byes.

(CHARLES' *face shows his annoyance at the interruption to his studies and he lies back on the sofa*)

CHARLES. Bedtime already?

JEAN. After six. How are you getting along? (*She pushes the pram up* R *of the sofa*)

CHARLES. Miles behind. Endless interruptions. It was idiotic to come back to this place. I should have remembered what it was like from the last time. We could have borrowed David's cottage . . .

JEAN. Nasty air in the Thames Valley. Not good for baby. Bournemouth air much better—(*to the baby*) isn't it, my little lammykins? He says, Yes, Mummy, lovely air, lovely sun, makes baby teep like an ickle top.

CHARLES. He doesn't say anything of the sort. All he ever appears to say is "goo". I'm getting a bit worried.

JEAN. Don't be silly, darling. What do you expect at five months —T. S. Eliot?

CHARLES. I think all this "tum along" stuff you smother him in is bad for him. It's very dangerous, too, you know. It can lead to arrested development later on.

(JEAN *moves* L *of the sofa and sits on the left side of it, with her back to the audience*)

JEAN (*complacently*) What nonsense you do talk (*She kisses him fondly*)

(CHARLES *does not respond*)

Give me a proper kiss. (*She pulls him into a sitting position*)

CHARLES (*murmuring*) A kiss, but not a tiss. (*He kisses her with a little more warmth, then breaks off and leans back*)

JEAN. Go on.

CHARLES. No.

JEAN. Why not?

CHARLES. It's too early.

JEAN (*rising, moving above the sofa and leaning over with her chin on his head*) You're so horribly coarse-grained sometimes that I wonder why I love you so much. But I do, you know, that's the awful thing. I've been thinking all the afternoon how much I loved you. Funny how it seems sort of to have crept up on me like this—did it creep up on you, too, or did you lie in your teeth before we got married?

CHARLES. I lied in my teeth. Now take baby up to beddy-byes, dear, and leave daddy to his worky-perky—or daddy won't ever become a docky-wocky.

(MAJOR POLLOCK'S *loud jovial voice is heard off in the garden*)

MAJOR (*off*) Hullo, 'ullo, Miss Meacham. Working out the form, eh? Got any tips for tomorrow?

MISS MEACHAM (*off*) I'll see.

CHARLES. Oh, God! Here's the Major.

(JEAN *moves to the pram*)

Go on, darling, for heaven's sake. If he sees the baby we're lost. He'll talk for hours about infant welfare in Polynesia or something.

JEAN. All right. (*To the baby*) Tum along, then. (*She meets Charle's eyes. Firmly*) Come along then, Vincent Michael Charles. It is time for your bath and subsequently for your bed. (*To Charles*) Better?

MISS MEACHAM (*off*) "Red Robin" in the three-thirty.

CHARLES. Much. (*He blows Jean a kiss*)

(JEAN *exits with the pram up* R. *A faint wail emerges from the pram*)

JEAN (*as she goes*) Oh. Did mummy bring him out of 'ovely garden into nasty dark p'ace? Naughty mummy. (*Her voice subsides*)

(CHARLES *returns to his book*)

MAJOR (*off*) "Red Robin" in the three-thirty? I'll remember that. Not that I can afford much these days, you know. Not like the old days when one would ring up the hall porter at *White's* and get him to put on a couple of ponies. Lovely day, what?

MISS MEACHAM (*off*) Not bad.

(MAJOR POLLOCK *enters by the french windows. He is in the*

middle fifties, with a clipped military moustache and extremely neat clothes. In fact, both in dress and appearance he is almost too exact a replica of the retired major to be entirely true. He carries two library books)

MAJOR. Hullo, Stratton. Still at it?

CHARLES *(with only the most perfunctory look-up from his book)* Yes, Major.

MAJOR. Don't know how you do it. Really don't. Most praiseworthy effort, I think. *(He puts the books on the desk)*

CHARLES. Thank you, Major.

(There is a pause as the MAJOR *crosses to the armchair* RC *and sits)*

MAJOR. Of course when I was at Sandhurst . . . Oh, so sorry—mustn't disturb you, must I?

CHARLES *(politely lowering his book)* That's all right, Major. When you were at Sandhurst?

MAJOR *(taking his pipe and pouch from his pocket)* Well, I was going to say that I was a bit like you. Off duty, while most of the other young fellers were gallivanting about in town, I used to be up in my room, or in the library there, cramming away like mad. Military history—great battles of the world—Clausewitz—that sort of stuff. I could have told you quite a lot about Clausewitz once.

CHARLES. Oh. And you can't now?

MAJOR. No. Afraid not. Everything goes, you know. Everything goes. Still I didn't regret all those hours of study at the time. I did jolly well at Sandhurst.

CHARLES. Did you get the Sword of Honour?

MAJOR. What? No. Came quite close to it, though. Passed out pretty high. Pretty high. Not that it did much good later on—except that they made me battalion adjutant because I was good at paper work. Could have been brigade major as it happens. Turned it down because I thought, if trouble came—well—you know—miles behind the line—away from one's own chaps. I suppose it was a bit foolish. I'd probably have been a general now, on full pay. Promotion was always a bit tight in the Black Watch. Should have chosen another regiment, I suppose.

CHARLES *(plainly hoping to terminate the conversation)* Yes.

MAJOR. Go on, my boy. Go on. So sorry. I talk too much. That's usually the trouble with old retired majors, what?

CHARLES. Not at all, sir. But I *will* go on, if you don't mind. I've rather a lot to do.

(There is a pause during which the MAJOR *lights and puffs at his pipe.* CHARLES *continues reading. After a few moments the* MAJOR *rises and, taking infinite pains not to make a sound, tiptoes to the desk, picks up one of his books, tiptoes back to the*

armchair RC *and resumes his seat.* CHARLES *has plainly been
aware of the Major's tactfully silent passage.*

FOWLER *enters by the french windows. He carries an
opened letter)*

FOWLER. Oh, hullo, Major. I've just had the most charming
letter . . .

MAJOR *(putting his fingers to his lips and indicating Charles)*
Ssh!

(FOWLER *sits at the desk and writes.* CHARLES *rises resignedly
and moves above the Major's chair)*

Oh, I say! I do hope we're not driving you away.

CHARLES. No, that's quite all right. I can always concentrate
much better in my room.

MAJOR. But you've got the baby up there, haven't you?

CHARLES. Yes, but it's a very quiet baby. It hasn't learnt to talk
yet.

(CHARLES *exits up* R)

MAJOR. Well, Fowler, who's your letter from? An old flame?

FOWLER *(turning in his chair and chuckling happily)* Old flame?
I haven't got any old flames. I leave that to you galloping majors.

MAJOR. Well, I used to do all right once, I must say. In the
regiment they used to call me Bucko Pollock. Regency buck—
you see. Still those days are past and gone. *Eheu fugaces—postume,
postume.*

FOWLER *(correcting his accent) Eheu fugaces, postume postume.*
Didn't they teach you the new pronunciation at Wellington?

MAJOR. No. The old.

FOWLER. When were you there?

MAJOR. Now let's think. It must have been nineteen-eighteen
I went up.

FOWLER. But they were using the new pronunciation then, I
know. Our head classics master was an old Wellingtonian, and I
remember distinctly his telling me . . .

MAJOR. Well, perhaps they did, and I've forgotten it. Never was
much of a hand at Greek.

FOWLER *(over the back of his chair; shocked)* Latin. *Horace.*

MAJOR. *Horace,* of course. Stupid of me. *(He laughs and puts
his pipe in the ashtray on the coffee table. Plainly changing the
subject)* Well, who is your letter from?

FOWLER *(facing down stage)* It's a boy who used to be in my
house and I haven't heard from for well over ten years. Brilliant
boy he was, and done very well since. I can't think how he knew I
was down here. Very good of him, I must say.

MAJOR. What happened to that other ex-pupil of yours—the
painter feller?

FOWLER. Oh. I still read about him in the newspapers occasionally. But I'm afraid I don't get much personal news of him. We've—rather lost touch, lately. (*He resumes his writing*)

(MISS COOPER *enters up* R. *She carries a newspaper under her arm and a vase of flowers which she puts on the table up* C)

MISS COOPER. Good afternoon, Major. (*She moves to* L *of the Major's chair*)
MAJOR (*rising*) Good afternoon, Miss Cooper.
MISS COOPER. We've managed to get your *West Hampshire Weekly News*. (*She hands the newspaper to the Major*) Joe had to go to three places before he could find one.
MAJOR. Thank you very much.
MISS COOPER. What was the urgency?
MAJOR. Oh—I just wanted to have a look at it, you know. I've never read it—strange to say—although I've been here—what is it—four years?
MISS COOPER. I'm not surprised. There's never anything in it except parking offences and cattle shows.
MAJOR. Thanks, anyway. (*He turns away from her, sits on the left arm of his chair and opens the paper*)

(*The* MAJOR, *during the ensuing lines between* MISS COOPER *and* FOWLER *and unseen by them, turns the pages of his paper over quickly as if he was searching for something. Suddenly his eye is evidently caught by what he reads, and he folds the paper back with a sharp sound.* MISS COOPER *moves to the table up* C, *sets the new vase in place and picks up the one previously there*)

FOWLER. I've had a charming letter, Miss Cooper, from someone I haven't seen or heard from in over ten years.
MISS COOPER (*brightly*) How nice. I'm so glad.
FOWLER. I'm going to write to him and ask him if he'd care to come down for a day or two. Of course he probably won't—but just in case he does, will that room be vacant?
MISS COOPER. Not at the moment, I'm afraid, Mr Fowler. We have so many casuals. But at the end of September . . .
FOWLER. Good. I'll ask him for then.

(MISS COOPER *exits with the old flowers into the dining-room*)

(*Still writing*) You were with the Highland Division at Alamein, weren't you, Major?

(*The* MAJOR *does not reply*)

Major—I said—you were with the Highland Division at Alamein?

(*There is no immediate reply. When the* MAJOR *does look up, his eyes are glassy and staring*)

MAJOR. What? No. No, I wasn't. Not with the Highland Division.

FOWLER (*looking at him*) I thought you were.

MAJOR (*almost fiercely*) I never said so.

FOWLER. (*putting his letter in an envelope*) I just wondered, because this boy—Macleod his name is—James, I think, or John —(*he picks up his hat and rises*) anyway he was known at school as Curly—he says in this letter he was with the Highland Division. I just wondered if you'd run into him at all.

MAJOR. Macleod? No. No, I don't think so.

FOWLER. Well, of course it would have been very unlikely if you had. (*He licks and seals the envelope*) It was just possible, though. (*He crosses to the arch up* R)

(*The* MAJOR *holds his paper and stares blankly into space*)

(*To himself*) Curly Macleod. He once elided a whole word in his Greek Iambics.

(FOWLER, *chuckling to himself, exits up* R.

MISS COOPER *enters from the dining-room, moves to the desk, picks up the waste-paper basket and moves to the table down* L. *The* MAJOR *looks down at his paper and pretends to be reading it casually*)

MAJOR. Yes. Pretty dull, I grant you.

MISS COOPER. What? (*She empties the ashtray from the table down* L *into the waste-paper basket*)

MAJOR. This paper. I don't suppose it's much read, is it?

MISS COOPER (*crossing to the coffee table in front of the fireplace*) Only by locals, I suppose. Farmers, estate agents—those sort of people. (*She empties the ashtray*)

MAJOR. I've never heard of anyone in the hotel reading it— have you?

MISS COOPER. Oh, yes. Mrs Railton-Bell takes it every week.

MAJOR. Does she? Whatever for?

MISS COOPER (*crossing below the sofa and replacing the waste-basket by the desk*) I don't know, I'm sure. There's not a lot that goes on in the world—even in West Hampshire—that she likes to miss. And she can afford fourpence for the information, I suppose.

MAJOR (*laughing jovially*) Yes, I suppose so. Funny though— I've never seen her reading it.

MISS COOPER (*crossing to the fireplace*) Oh, she gets a lot of things sent in to her that she never reads. (*She collects an empty cigarette packet from the hearth*) Most of the stuff on that table over there is hers. (*She crosses and puts the packet in the waste-paper basket*)

MAJOR. Yes. Yes, I know. She'd have had hers this morning then, I suppose?

MISS COOPER. Yes. I suppose so.

Major. Oh. Dash it all. Here I've gone and spent fourpence for nothing. I mean, I could have borrowed hers, couldn't I? (*He laughs heartily*)

(Miss Cooper *smiles politely and, having finished her tidying, moves towards the arch up* R)

Miss Cooper (*pausing*) I know you don't like venison, Major, so I've ordered you a chop for lunch tomorrow. Only I must ask you to be discreet about it, if you don't mind.

Major. Yes, of course. Of course. Thank you so much, Miss Cooper.

(Miss Cooper *exits up* R. *The* Major *opens the paper quickly and stares at it for some time, reading avidly. Then he suddenly rips out the whole page, crumpling it up and thrusting it into his pocket. He folds the remains of the paper and puts it on the seat of the armchair* RC. *He then moves quickly to the table up* C *and after a feverish search, finds the "West Hampshire Weekly News". He puts the paper on the end of the sofa and opens it to find the evidently offending page.*

Mrs Railton-Bell *enters up* R *and moves to* R *of the table up* C.

Sibyl Railton-Bell. *her daughter, follows her on. She is a timid-looking, wizened creature in the late thirties, bespectacled, dowdy, and without make-up*)

Mrs Railton-Bell (*as she enters*) Well, if that's what you meant you should have said so, dear. I wish you'd learn to express yourself a little bit better. Good afternoon, Major Pollock.

Major. Good afternoon, Mrs Railton-Bell. (*To Sibyl. Jovially*) Afternoon, Miss R.B.

(Sibyl *stands in front of the table up* C. *The* Major *is holding the paper, unable to hide it or put it back on the table. He sees that* Mrs Railton-Bell *has noticed it*)

I'm so sorry. I was just glancing through your *West Hampshire News*. I wonder if you'd let me borrow it for a few moments? There's something in it I want to see.

Mrs Railton-Bell. Very well, Major. Only please return it. (*She moves to the armchair* RC)

Major. Of course. (*He moves to the french windows*)

(Mrs Railton-Bell *picks up the Major's copy of the paper from the chair* RC)

Mrs Railton-Bell. Oh—Major—here's another copy.

Major (*turning; feigning astonishment*) Of the *West Hampshire Weekly News*?

Mrs Railton-Bell. Yes.

Major. Well, I'm dashed!

MRS RAILTON-BELL. It was over here— on the chair.

MAJOR. Must be one of the casuals, I suppose.

MRS RAILTON-BELL (*straightening the paper*) You'd better take it anyway, and leave me mine.

MAJOR (*doubtfully*) You don't think, whoever owns it, might . . .?

MRS RAILTON-BELL (*moving towards him*) If it's been left on the chair, it's plainly been read. I'd like mine back, if you don't mind, please, Major..

MAJOR (*conceding defeat*) Righty-oh. I'll put it back with the others. (*He puts the paper on the table up* C *and takes the other copy from Mrs Railton-Bell*) Well—think I'll just go out for a little stroll. (*He moves to the french windows*)

SIBYL (*shyly*) You don't happen to want company, do you, Major Pollock? I haven't had my walk yet.

MAJOR (*turning to Sibyl; embarrassed*) Well, Miss R.B.—jolly nice suggestion and all that—the only thing is I'm going to call on a friend—you see—and . . .

(MRS RAILTON-BELL *sits in the easy chair above the fireplace*)

SIBYL (*more embarrassed than the Major*) Oh, yes, yes. Of course. I'm so sorry.

MAJOR. No, no. I'm the one who's sorry. Well, cheery-bye till dinner.

(*The* MAJOR *exits by the french windows*)

MRS RAILTON-BELL. I wish he wouldn't use that revolting expression. It's so common. But then he *is* common.

SIBYL. Oh no, Mummy. Do you think so? He was in a very good regiment.

MRS RAILTON-BELL. You can be in the Horse Guards and still be common, dear.

(SIBYL *moves to* L *of Mrs Railton-Bell*)

(*Gently*) Sibyl, my dearest, do you mind awfully if your tactless old mother whispers something in your ear?

SIBYL (*resigned*) No.

MRS RAILTON-BELL. I didn't think it was *terribly* wise of you to lay yourself open to that snub just now.

SIBYL. It wasn't a snub, Mummy. I'm sure he really *was* going to see a friend.

(MRS RAILTON-BELL *smiles understandingly and sympathetically, shaking her head ever so slightly*)

Well, I often *do* go for walks with the Major.

MRS RAILTON-BELL. I know you do, dear. What is more, quite a lot of people have noticed it.

(*There is a pause.* SIBYL *stares at her mother*)

Sibyl (*at length*) You don't mean—you can't mean . . . (*She holds her cheeks with a sudden gesture*) Oh, no. How can people be so awful! (*She moves to* R *of the armchair* RC *and turns to Mrs Railton-Bell*)

Mrs Railton-Bell. It's not being particularly awful when an unattached girl is noticed constantly seeking the company of an attractive older man.

Sibyl (*still holding her cheeks*) They think I chase him. Is that it? They think I run after him, they think I want him to . . . (*She turns up* C *with her hand to her mouth*) They think . . . (*She moves to the chair* RC *and sits*) No, it *is* awful. It *is*. It *is*.

Mrs Railton-Bell (*sharply*) Quieten yourself, my dear. Don't get into one of your *states,* now.

Sibyl. It's all right, Mummy. I'm not in a state. It's just—well —it's just so dreadful that people should believe such a thing is even possible. I hate that side of life. I hate it.

Mrs Railton-Bell (*soothingly*) I know you do, dear. But it exists all the same, and one has to be very careful in this world not to give people the wrong impression. Quieter now?

Sibyl. Yes, Mummy.

Mrs Railton-Bell. Good. (*She rises and moves to* L *of Sibyl, putting a hand on her shoulder for a moment as she passes*) You must try not to let these things upset you so much, dear.

Sibyl. I only go for walks with the Major because I like hearing him talk. I like all his stories about London and the war and the regiment—and—well—he's seen so much of life and I haven't.

Mrs Railton-Bell (*moving down* R *of the sofa*) I don't know what you mean by that, dear, I'm sure.

Sibyl. I only meant . . . (*She checks herself*)

(Mrs Railton-Bell *turns to Sibyl*)

I'm sorry.

Mrs Railton-Bell (*sitting on the right side of the sofa; relentlessly pursuing her prey*) Of course I realize that you must occasionally miss some of the gaieties of life—the balls and the cocktail parties and things—that a few other lucky young people can enjoy. I can assure you, dearest, if I could possibly afford it, you'd have them. (*She reaches out her hand to Sibyl*) But I *do* do my best, you know.

Sibyl (*taking her mother's hand*) I know you do, Mummy. (*She withdraws her hand*)

Mrs Railton-Bell. There was Rome last year, and our Scandinavian cruise the year before . . .

Sibyl. I know, Mummy. I know. Don't think I'm not grateful. Please. It's only . . . (*She breaks off*)

Mrs Railton-Bell (*gently prompting*) Only what, dear?

Sibyl. If only I could *do* something. After all, I'm thirty-three.

Mrs Railton-Bell. No, my dear. We've been over this so often.

Dearest child, you'd never stand any job for more than a few weeks. Remember Jones & Jones.

SIBYL. But that was because I had to work in a basement, and I used to feel stifled and faint. But there must be something else.

MRS RAILTON-BELL (*gently patting her hand*) You're not a very strong child, dear. You must get that into your head. Your nervous system isn't nearly as sound as it should be.

SIBYL. You mean my *states*? But I haven't had one of those for a long time.

MRS RAILTON-BELL. No dear—you've been doing very well. Very well indeed. But there's quite a big difference between not having hysterical fits and being strong enough to take a job. (*Concluding the topic decisively*) Now hand me that newspaper, would you, dear?

SIBYL. (*rising*) Which one?

MRS RAILTON-BELL. The *West Hampshire Weekly News.* I want to see what the Major was so interested in.

(SIBYL *moves to the table up* C, *gets the newspaper, hands it to Mrs Railton-Bell, then sits in the easy chair above the fireplace, puts on her spectacles and reads her book*)

(*She fumbles in her bag*) Oh dear me, what a silly billy. I've gone and left my glasses and my book in the shelter at the end of Ragusa Road. Oh dear, I do hope they're not stolen. I expect they're bound to be. Now—doesn't that show how dependent I am on you, my dear? If you hadn't had that headache you'd have been with me this afternoon, and then you'd never have allowed me to . . .

SIBYL (*rising*) I'll go and look for them. (*She puts her book on the table up* C *and moves to the french windows*)

MRS RAILTON-BELL. Oh, would you, dear? That really is so kind of you. I hate you to fetch and carry for me, as you know— but my old legs are just a wee bit tired—it was the far end of the shelter, facing the sea.

SIBYL (*turning in the windows*) Where we usually sit? I know.

(SIBYL *exits by the french windows.* MRS RAILTON-BELL *looks at the paper, holds it at arm's length, then with a sigh of impatience, rises, moves to the french windows, and holds the paper open in the sunlight and tries to read it.*

LADY MATHESON *enters up* R *and moves above the easy chair*)

LADY MATHESON. Oh, hullo, dear. It's nearly time for the news-reel.

MRS RAILTON-BELL (*in a strained voice*) Gladys, have you got your glasses?

LADY MATHESON. Yes, I think so. (*She feels in her bag*) Yes, here they are. (*She crosses to* R *of Mrs Railton-Bell*)

Mrs Railton-Bell. Then read this out to me. (*She hands the paper to Lady Matheson and indicates the item*)

(Lady Matheson *puts on her spectacles*)

Lady Matheson (*unsuspecting*) Where, dear? (*she reads*) "Lorry driver loses licence"?

Mrs Railton-Bell. No, no. "Ex-officer bound over."

Lady Matheson (*brightly*) Oh, yes. (*She reads*) "Ex-officer bound over. Offence in cinema." (*She looks up*) In cinema? Oh dear—do we really want to hear this?

Mrs Railton-Bell (*crossing below the sofa to* R *of it; grimly*) Yes. Yes, we do. (*She sits on the sofa*) Go on.

Lady Matheson (*with a step in; reading resignedly*) "On Thursday last, before the Bournemouth magistrates, David Angus Pollock, fifty-five, giving his address as—(*she starts violently*) the *Beauregard Hotel,* Morgan Crescent . . ." (*In a feverish whisper*) Major Pollock! Oh!

Mrs Railton-Bell. Go on.

Lady Matheson (*reading*) ". . . Morgan Crescent—pleaded guilty to a charge of insulting behaviour in a Bournemouth cinema . . ." Oh! Oh! ". . . on the complaint of a Mrs Osborn, forty-three—(*breathlessly*) of four Studland Road." He must have been drinking.

Mrs Railton-Bell. He's a teetotaller.

Lady Matheson. Perhaps just that one night . . .

Mrs Railton-Bell. No. Read on.

Lady Matheson (*reading*) "Mrs Osborn, giving evidence, stated that Pollock, sitting next to her, persistently nudged her in the arm, and later attempted to take other liberties. She subsequently vacated her seat, and complained to an usherette. Inspector Franklin, giving evidence, said that in response to a telephone call from the cinema manager, Pollock had been kept under observation by police officers from three fifty-three p.m. until seven-ten p.m. by which time he had been observed to change his seat no less than five times, always choosing a seat next to a female person. (*She moves slowly above the sofa*) ~~There had, he admitted, been no further complaints, but that was not unusual in cases of this kind.~~ On leaving the cinema Pollock was arrested and after being charged and cautioned, stated: 'You have made a terrible mistake. You have the wrong man. I was only in the place half an hour. I am a colonel in the Scots Guards.' Later he made a statement. Appearing on behalf of the defendant, Mr William Crowther, solicitor, stated that his client had had a momentary aberration. He was extremely sorry and ashamed of himself and would undertake never to behave in so stupid and improper a manner in future. He asked that his client's blameless record should be taken into account. He had enlisted in the army in nineteen twenty-five and in nineteen thirty-nine was granted a commission as second lieutenant in the Royal Army Service Corps." (*She moves to the armchair* RC *and sits*)

MRS RAILTON-BELL. Any more?

LADY MATHESON (*reading*) "During the war he had held a responsible position in charge of an Army Supply Depot in the Orkney Islands and had been discharged in nineteen forty-six with the rank of full lieutenant. Pollock was not called. The chairman of the Bench, giving judgement, said: 'You have behaved disgustingly, but because this appears to be your first offence we propose to deal leniently with you.' The defendant was bound over for twelve months." (*She lowers the paper, disturbed and flustered to the core of her being*) Oh, dear. Oh, dear. Oh, dear.

MRS RAILTON-BELL (*perfectly composed but excited*) Thursday. It must have happened on Wednesday. Do you remember—he missed dinner that night?

LADY MATHESON. Did he? Yes, so he did. Oh, dear. It's all too frightful. I can hardly believe it. Persistently! It's so dreadful.

MRS RAILTON-BELL. On the Thursday he was terribly nervous and depressed. I remember now. And then on the Friday suddenly as bright as a button. Of course he must have read the papers next day and thought he'd got away with it. What a stroke of luck that I get this weekly one sent to me.

LADY MATHESON. Luck, dear? Is it luck?

MRS RAILTON-BELL. Of course it's luck. Otherwise we'd never have known.

LADY MATHESON. Wouldn't that have been better?

MRS RAILTON-BELL. Gladys! What are you saying?

LADY MATHESON. I don't know—oh, dear. I'm so fussed and confused. No, of course it wouldn't have been better. One has to know these things, I suppose—although sometimes I wonder why.

MRS RAILTON-BELL. Because if there's a liar and a fraudulent crook and a—I can't bring myself to say it—wandering around among us unsuspected, there could be—well—there could be the most terrible repercussions.

LADY MATHESON. Well, he's been wandering around among us for four years now and there haven't been any repercussions yet. (*With a faint sigh*) I suppose we're too old.

MRS RAILTON-BELL (*coldly*) I have a daughter, you know.

LADY MATHESON. Oh. Poor Sibyl. Yes. And she's such a friend of his, isn't she? Oh, dear.

MRS RAILTON-BELL. Exactly.

LADY MATHESON (*after a moment's troubled reflection*) Maud, dear—it's not my business, I know, and of course you have a mother's duty to protect your child, that of course I do see—and yet—well—she's such a strange girl—so excitable and shy—and so ungrown-up in so many ways . . .

MRS RAILTON-BELL. Come to the point, Gladys.

Lady Matheson. Yes, I will. It's this. I don't think you ought to tell her.

Mrs Railton-Bell. Not *tell* her?

Lady Matheson. Well, not all of it. Not the details. Say he's a fraud, if you like, but not—please, Maud—not about the cinema. (*Suddenly distressed by the thought herself*) Oh, dear! I don't know how I shall ever look him in the face again.

Mrs Railton-Bell. You won't have to, dear. (*She rises purposefully and moves to L of the sofa*) I'm going to see Miss Cooper now and insist that he leaves this hotel before dinner tonight.

Lady Matheson. Oh, dear. I wonder if you should?

Mrs Railton-Bell. Gladys, what *has* come over you this evening? Of course I should.

Lady Matheson. But you know what Miss Cooper is—so independent and stubborn sometimes, She might not agree.

Mrs Railton-Bell. Of course she'll agree. She *has* to agree if we all insist.

Lady Matheson. But we don't *all*. I mean it's just the two of us. Shouldn't we consult the others first? (*Suddenly realizing the implication*) Oh, gracious! Of course that means we'll have to tell them all, doesn't it?

Mrs Railton-Bell (*moving above the sofa; delighted*) An excellent idea, Gladys. Where's Mr Fowler?

Lady Matheson. In his room, I think.

Mrs Railton-Bell (*moving to L of Lady Matheson*) And the young people? Shall we have them? They count as regulars by now, I suppose. Yes. We'll have them, too.

Lady Matheson. Oh, dear. I hate telling tales.

Mrs Railton-Bell. Telling tales? (*she points dramatically to the "West Hampshire Weekly News"*) The tale is told already, Gladys— to the world. (*She takes the paper from Lady Matheson*)

Lady Matheson. Well, strictly speaking—only to West Hampshire.

Mrs Railton-Bell. Don't quibble, Gladys. (*She moves above the sofa to the french windows*) Miss Meacham's in the garden. I really don't think we need bother about Miss Meacham. She's so odd and unpredictable—and getting odder and more unpredictable every day. (*She looks out of the window*) Here comes Sibyl. Go up and get the others down, dear.

(Lady Matheson *rises*)

(*She moves above the sofa*) I'll deal with her.

Lady Matheson (*moving to the arch up R*) Maud, you won't . . . You'll remember what I said, won't you?

Mrs Railton-Bell. Yes, of course. Go on, dear.

(Lady Matheson *exits up R*.
    Sibyl *enters by the french windows and moves to L of the sofa. She carries a book and a spectacle case*)

(*She moves to* R *of the sofa. To Sibyl*) You found them, did you, darling? Clever girl. (*She picks up her bag from the sofa, then takes the book and glasses from Sibyl*)

(*There is a pause, during which* Mrs Railton-Bell *sits in the armchair* RC *and* Sibyl *sits on the sofa at the left side*)

(*At length*) Sibyl, dear. I think you'd better go to your room if you don't mind.

Sibyl (*rising*) Why, Mummy?

Mrs Railton-Bell. We're holding a meeting of the regulars down here to discuss a very urgent matter that has just cropped up.

Sibyl (*kneeling on the sofa*) Oh, but how exciting! Can't I stay? After all, I'm a regular, too.

Mrs Railton-Bell. I know, dear, but I doubt if the subject of the meeting is quite suitable for you.

Sibyl. Why, Mummy? What is it?

Mrs Railton-Bell. Oh, dear! You're such an inquisitive child. Very well, then. I'll tell you this much—but only this much. We are going to discuss whether or not we think Miss Cooper should be told to ask Major Pollock to leave this hotel at once and never come back .

Sibyl (*aghast*) What? But I don't understand. Why Mummy?

(Mrs Railton-Bell *does not reply*)

Mummy, tell me, why?

Mrs Railton-Bell. I can't tell you, dear. It might upset you too much.

Sibyl. But I must know, Mummy. I must. What has he done?

Mrs Railton-Bell (*after only the slightest hesitation*) You really *insist* I should tell you?

Sibyl. Yes, I do.

Mrs Railton-Bell. Even after my strong warning?

Sibyl. Yes.

Mrs Railton-Bell (*with a sigh*) Very well then, dear. I have no option, I suppose. (*With a quick gesture she hands the paper to Sibyl*) Read that. Middle column. Half-way down. "Ex-officer bound over."

(Sibyl *rises, puts on her glasses, moves slowly to the desk chair, sits and reads the report.* Mrs Railton-Bell *watches her.* Sibyl *drops the paper on to her lap, removes her glasses and sits, her eyes staring, but her face blank.*

Lady Matheson *enters up* R. *She sees Sibyl instantly and moves to the fireplace*)

Lady Matheson (*as she enters*) The others are just coming. (*Shocked*) Oh, Maud, you haven't . . .

Mrs Railton-Bell. I did my best. dear, but she insisted. She absolutely insisted. (*She rises, moves to* R *of Sibyl and bends solicitously over her*) I'm so sorry, my dear.

(SIBYL *puts the paper on the desk*)

It must be a dreadful shock for you. It was for us too, as you can imagine. Are you all right?

(SIBYL *makes no reply*)

(*Slightly more sharply*) Are you all right, Sibyl?
SIBYL (*barely audible*) Yes, Mummy.

(LADY MATHESON *sits in the chair down* R.

JEAN *enters up* R, *looking rather annoyed. She carries a baby's nightdress, a bodkin and a ribbon*)

JEAN (*crossing to the settee* L) What is it, Mrs Railton-Bell? I can only stay a moment. I must get back to the baby.
MRS RAILTON-BELL. I won't keep you long, I promise. Kindly take a seat, please.

(JEAN *sits on the settee*)

(*She turns to Sibyl. Sharply*) Sibyl, what have you done?

(CHARLES *enters up* R)

(*She takes Sibyl's glasses from her hand*) Look, you've broken your your glasses.
SIBYL (*murmuring*) How stupid.
CHARLES (*moving to Sibyl*) Hullo, you've cut your hand, haven't you?
SIBYL. No.
CHARLES. Yes, you have. Let's see. (*With a rather professional air he picks up her limp hand and examines it*) Nothing much. No splinters. Here, you'd better have this. (*He takes a clean handkerchief from his breast pocket*) It's quite clean. (*He ties the handkerchief neatly round her hand*) Iodine and a bit of plaster later.

(FOWLER *enters up* R)

MRS RAILTON-BELL (*crossing below the sofa to the armchair* RC *and sitting*) Ah, Mr Fowler, good. Would you take a seat, and then we can begin.

(FOWLER *sits in the easy chair*)

The two young people are in a hurry. Now, ladies and gentlemen, I'm afraid I have very grave news for you all.
CHARLES (*perching himself on the upstage end of the sofa*) The boiler's wrong again?

(SIBYL, *during the whole of the following discussions, does not*

*stir in her chair. Her two hands, one bound with a handkerchief,
rest motionless in her lap, and she stares at the wall opposite her)*

MRS RAILTON-BELL. No. I only wish it were something so trivial.

CHARLES. I don't consider shaving in cold brown water trivial.

MRS RAILTON-BELL. Please, Mr Stratton.

FOWLER (*anxiously*) They're raising the prices again?

MRS RAILTON-BELL. No. My news is graver even than that.

FOWLER. I don't know what could be graver than that.

MRS RAILTON-BELL. The news I have to give you, Mr Fowler...

CHARLES. Look, Mrs Railton-Bell must we play Twenty
Questions? Can't you just tell us what it is?

MRS RAILTON-BELL (*angrily*) My hesitation is only because the
matter is so painful and so embarrassing for me that I find it
difficult to choose my words. However, if you want it boldly, you
shall have it. (*After a dramatic pause*) Major Pollock—who is not
a major at all, but a lieutenant promoted from the ranks in the
R.A.S.C. ...

CHARLES (*excitedly*) No! You don't say! I knew it, you know.
I always knew Sandhurst and the Black Watch was a phoney.
Didn't I say so, Jean?

JEAN. Yes, you did, but I said it first—that night he made the
boob about serviettes.

FOWLER (*chipping in quickly*) I must admit I've always slightly
suspected the public school education; I mean, only today he
made the most shocking mistake in quoting *Horace*—quite appal-
ling. I mean he actually thought ...

MRS RAILTON-BELL (*raising her voice*) Please, please, please,
ladies and gentlemen. This is not the point. The dreadful, the
really ghastly revelation is still to come. (*She gains silence, and
once again pauses dramatically*) He was found guilty ...

LADY MATHESON. Pleaded guilty.

MRS RAILTON-BELL. Gladys. He was found or pleaded guilty—
I don't really see that it matters which—to behaving insultingly
to no less than six respectable women in a Bournemouth cinema.

(*There is an aghast silence*)

CHARLES (*at length*) Good God! What a performance.

LADY MATHESON. Really, Maud, I must correct that. I must.
We only know one was respectable—the one who complained—
and even she seemed a little odd in her behaviour. Why didn't
she just say straight out to the Major: 'I do wish you'd stop doing
whatever it is that you are doing"? That's what I'd have done.
About the other five we don't know anything at all. We don't
even know if he nudged them or anything.

MRS RAILTON-BELL. Of course he nudged them. He was in that
cinema for an immoral purpose—he admitted it. And he was seen
to change seat five times—always choosing one next to female
persons.

CHARLES. That could make ten nudges, really, couldn't it? If he had the chance of using both elbows.

JEAN. Eleven, with the original one. Or twelve, supposing . . .

MRS RAILTON-BELL. Really, we seem to be losing the essential point in a welter of trivialities. The point is surely that the Major —the so-called Major—has pleaded guilty to a criminal offence of a disgusting nature, and I want to know what action we regular residents propose to take.

FOWLER. What action do you propose, Mrs Railton-Bell?

MRS RAILTON-BELL. I propose, on your behalf, to go to Miss Cooper and demand that he leaves the hotel forthwith.

CHARLES. No.

MRS RAILTON-BELL. You disagree, Mr Stratton?

CHARLES. Yes, I do. Please don't think I'm making light of this business, Mrs Railton-Bell. To me, what he's done, if he's done it, seems ugly and repulsive. I've always had an intense dislike of the more furtive forms of sexual expression. So emotionally I'm entirely on your side. But logically I'm not.

MRS RAILTON-BELL (*cuttingly*) Are you making a speech, Mr Stratton? If so, perhaps you'd like to stand here and address us.

CHARLES. No. I'm all right where I am,· thank you. And I'm not making a speech, either. I'm just saying that my dislike of the Major's offence is emotional and not logical. My lack of understanding of it is probably a shortcoming in me. The Major presumably understands my form of lovemaking. I *should* therefore understand his. But I don't. So I am plainly in a state of prejudice against him, and must be very wary of any moral judgements I may pass in this matter. It's only fair to approach it from the purely logical standpoint of practical Christian ethics, and ask myself the question: "What harm has the man done?" Well, apart from possibly slightly bruising the arm of a certain lady, whose motives in complaining—I agree with Lady Matheson— are extremely questionable—apart from that, and apart from telling us a few rather pathetic lies about his past life, which most of us do anyway from time to time, I really can't see he's done anything to justify us chucking him out into the street.

JEAN (*hotly*) I don't agree at all. I feel disgusted at what he's done, too, but I think I'm quite right to feel disgusted. I don't consider myself prejudiced at all, and I think that people who behave like that are a public menace and deserve anything they get.

CHARLES. Your vehemence is highly suspect. I must have you psycho-analyzed.

JEAN. It's absolutely logical, Charles. Supposing next time it's a daughter . . .

CHARLES (*wearily*) I know. I know. And supposing in twenty or thirty years' time she sits next to a Major Pollock in a cinema . . .

JEAN. Exactly.

(CHARLES *laughs*)

It's not funny, Charles. How would you feel . . . ?

CHARLES. Very ashamed of her if she didn't use her elbows back, very hard, and in the right place.

JEAN (*rising*) Charles . . .

MRS RAILTON-BELL. Please, please, please. This is not a private argument between the two of you. I take it, Mr Stratton, you are against any action regarding this matter?

(CHARLES *nods*)

Of any kind at all?

(CHARLES *shakes his head*)

Not even in protest?

CHARLES. I might give him a reproving glance at dinner.

MRS RAILTON-BELL (*turning from him in disgust*) You, Mrs Stratton. I gather, agree with me that I should see Miss Cooper?

JEAN (*firmly*) Yes. (*She resumes her seat on the settee*)

CHARLES (*murmuring to Jean*) Book-burner. (*He rises and takes a step towards her*)

JEAN. (*furiously*) What's book-burning got to do with it?

CHARLES. A lot.

MRS RAILTON-BELL (*imperiously*) Quiet, please.

(CHARLES *sits on the sofa at the right side*)

(*She turns to Fowler*) Mr Fowler—what do you think?

FOWLER (*confused*) Well, it's difficult. Very difficult. I can't say I see it like Stratton. That's the modern viewpoint, I know—nothing is really wrong that doesn't do actual and accessible harm to another human being. But he's not correct when he calls that Christianity. Christianity, surely, goes much further than that. Certain acts are wrong because they are, in themselves and by themselves, impure and immoral, and it seems to me that this terrible wave of vice and sexual excess which seems to have flooded this country since the war might well, in part, be due to the decline of the old standards, emotional and illogical though they may well seem to the younger generation. Tolerance is not necessarily a good, you know. Tolerance of evil may itself be an evil. After all it was Aristotle, wasn't it, who said . . .

(MISS MEACHAM *enters by the french windows and moves to* L *of the sofa*)

MISS MEACHAM (*as she enters*) Oh, really! You've all gone too far too long about it. And when we start quoting Aristotle, well, personally, I'm going to my room. (*She crosses up* RC)

MRS RAILTON-BELL. You heard, Miss Meacham?

MISS MEACHAM. I couldn't help hearing. I didn't want to. I

was doing my system and you need to concentrate like billy-oh on that. (*She moves above the sofa*) I had my chair against the wall to catch the sun, and I certainly wasn't going to move into the cold just for you people.

MRS RAILTON-BELL. Well, as you know the facts, I suppose we should canvass your opinion. What is it?

MISS MEACHAM (*moving up* R) I haven't any.

MRS RAILTON-BELL. You must have *some* opinion.

MISS MEACHAM (*moving to* R *of Mrs Railton-Bell*) Why should I? I've been out of the world for far longer than any of you, and what do I know about morals and ethics? Only what I read in novels, and as I only read thrillers, that isn't worth much. In Peter Cheyney the hero does far worse things to his girls than the Major's done, and no-one seems to mind.

MRS RAILTON-BELL. I don't think that it's quite the point what Mr Cheyney's heroes do to his girls, Miss Meacham. We want your views on Major Pollock.

MISS MEACHAM. Do you? Well, my views on Major Pollock have always been that he's a crashing old bore, and a wicked old fraud. Now I hear he's a dirty old man, too, I'm not at all surprised, and quite between these four walls, I don't give a damn.

(MISS MEACHAM *exits up* R. *There is a pause, then* MRS RAILTON-BELL *turns to Fowler*)

MRS RAILTON-BELL. Sad, very sad. Well, Mr Fowler—I take it you are on the side of action?

(*There is a pause*)

FOWLER. I once had to recommend a boy for expulsion. Only once, in the whole of the fifteen years I was a housemaster. I was deeply unhappy about it. Deeply. And yet events proved me right. He was no good. He became a thief and a blackmailer, and—oh—horrible things happened to him. Horrible. (*After a moment's pause*) Poor boy. He *had* a way with him . . .

MRS RAILTON-BELL (*impatiently*) are you in favour of action, Mr Fowler?

FOWLER (*unhappily*) Yes, I suppose so. Yes, I am.

MRS RAILTON-BELL (*to Lady Matheson*) And you, Gladys?

(LADY MATHESON *hesitates*)

You don't need to make a speech like the others, dear. Just say yes or no.

(*There is a pause*)

LADY MATHESON (*at length*) Oh, dear!

MRS RAILTON-BELL. Now don't shilly-shally, Gladys. You know perfectly well what you feel about all this dreadful vice that's going on all over the country. You've told me often how people like that should be locked up.

(*There is a pause*)

LADY MATHESON (*at length*) Oh, dear!

MRS RAILTON-BELL (*really impatient*) Oh, for heaven's sake, make up your mind, Gladys. Are you on the side of Mr Stratton and his defence of vice, or are you on the side of the Christian virtues like Mr Fowler, Mrs Stratton and myself?

CHARLES (*quietly*) I have never in my life heard a question more disgracefully begged. Senator McCarthy could use your talents, Mrs Railton-Bell.

MRS RAILTON-BELL (*turning to Charles*) Will you keep quiet! (*She turns to Lady Matheson*) Well, Gladys, which is it to be?

LADY MATHESON. I'm on your side, of course. Oh, dear.

MRS RAILTON-BELL (*to Charles*) Well, Mr Stratton—apart from Miss Meacham, who might be said to be neutral, the count appears now to be five to one against you.

CHARLES. *Five* to one?

MRS RAILTON-BELL. My daughter, of course, agrees with me.

CHARLES. How do you know?

MRS RAILTON-BELL. I know her feelings in this matter.

CHARLES. May we hear them from herself? (*He rises and moves to* R *of Sibyl*) Miss Railton-Bell. Miss Railton-Bell—could we hear your views?

(SIBYL *does not reply*)

MRS RAILTON-BELL. Mr Stratton is asking you a question, dear.

SIBYL. Yes, Mummy?

CHARLES. Could we hear your views?

SIBYL. My views?

MRS RAILTON-BELL (*clearly, as to a child*) On Major Pollock, dear. What action should we take about him?

(SIBYL *seems puzzled and makes no reply*)

(*To the others, in an aside*) It's a shock. (*To Sibyl*) You know what you've just read in that paper, dear? What do you think of it?

SIBYL (*in a whisper*) It made me sick.

MRS RAILTON-BELL. Of course it did, dear. That's how we all feel.

SIBYL (*her voice growing louder in a crescendo*) It made me sick. It made me sick. It made me sick. It made me sick. (*She rises*)

MRS RAILTON-BELL (*rising, moving quickly to Sibyl and embracing her*) Yes, dear. Yes. Don't fuss now, don't fuss. It's all right.

SIBYL (*burying her face in her mother's arms*) I don't feel well, Mummy. Can I go and lie down?

MRS RAILTON-BELL. Of course you can, dear. We can go into

the writing-room. Such a nice comfy sofa, and there's never any-one there. (*She leads Sibyl to the arch up* R) And don't fret any more, my dear. Try to forget the whole business. Make believe it never happened—that there never was such a person as Major Pollock. That's the way.

(MRS RAILTON-BELL *and* SIBYL *exit up* R. CHARLES *moves to* R *of the sofa*)

LADY MATHESON. She should never have told her like that. It was such a mistake.

CHARLES (*angrily*) I agree. If that girl doesn't end as a mental case it won't be the fault of her mother.

LADY MATHESON (*loyally*) Mr Stratton—I must say I consider that a quite outrageous way of twisting my remark. I used the word "mistake", and you have no right . . .

CHARLES. No, I haven't. I'm sorry. The comment was purely my own.

JEAN. It was *your* fault for asking her views.

CHARLES (*moving above the sofa to Jean*) She was sitting there quite peacefully, apparently listening. I wasn't to know she was in a state of high suppressed hysteria. I might, admittedly, have guessed, but anyway I had an idiotic but well-meaning hope that I might get her—just this once—just this once in the whole of her life—to disagree publicly with her mother. (*He crosses below the sofa and sits in the armchair* RC) It could save her soul if she ever did.

FOWLER. I didn't realize that modern psychiatry recognized so old-fashioned and sentimental a term as soul, Mr Stratton.

CHARLES. Very well, for soul read mind, and one day when you have a spare ten minutes explain to me the difference.

FOWLER. I will.

CHARLES (*rising and moving above the sofa*) Not now, I'm afraid. It might muddle my anatomical studies. (*To Jean*) Are you coming?

(JEAN *rises, rather reluctantly*)

JEAN. I don't know what's the matter with you this evening, Charles. You're behaving like an arrogant pompous boor.

CHARLES. You must forgive me. I suppose it's just that I'm feeling a little light-headed at finding myself, on an issue of common humanity, in a minority of one. The sin of spiritual pride, that's called— isn't it, Mr Fowler?

(CHARLES *exits up* R)

JEAN. He's been overworking, you know. He'll be quite different about all this tomorrow. (*Confidently*) I'll see to that. (*She sits on the left side of the sofa, with her back to the audience*)

(MRS RAILTON-BELL *enters up* R *and moves up* R *of the sofa*)

MRS RAILTON-BELL. She's quite all right, now. She always recovers from these little states very quickly. She's resting peacefully in the writing-room.

LADY MATHESON. Oh, good.

JEAN. I was about apologizing for my husband's behaviour, Mrs Railton-Bell.

MRS RAILTON-BELL. Thank you, my dear—but what I always say is—we're all of us entitled to our own opinions, however odd and dangerous and distasteful they may sometimes be. (*Briskly*) Now. Shall we all go and see Miss Cooper in a body, or would you rather I acted as your spokesman?

(*It is plain which course* MRS RAILTON-BELL *would prefer. After a pause, the others begin to murmur diffidently*)

JEAN		Oh, no.
LADY MATHESON		I think perhaps if *you* went.
	(*together*)	dear . . .
FOWLER		I don't think a deputation is
		a good idea.

JEAN. You be our spokesman.

MRS RAILTON-BELL. Very well. (*She picks up the copy of the newspaper from the desk and goes to the arch up* R) I hope you all understand it's a duty I hardly relish.

(MRS RAILTON-BELL *exits up* R)

FOWLER (*to Lady Matheson*) I would hardly call that a strictly accurate self-appraisal, would you?

LADY MATHESON (*doubtfully*) Well—after all—doing a duty can seem a pleasure, to some people, can't it? It never has done to me, I agree, but then I'm—well—so weak and silly about these things.

JEAN (*rising and crossing to the arch up* R) It would be a pleasure to me, too, in this case. Horrid old man. (*To herself, as she goes*) I hope the baby's not been crying.

(JEAN *exits up* R)

FOWLER. A ruthless young girl that, I should say.

LADY MATHESON. So many young people are these days, don't you think?

FOWLER (*meaningly*) Not only young people.

LADY MATHESON (*unhappily*) Yes—well. (*With a sigh*) Oh dear! What a dreadful affair. It's made me quite miserable.

FOWLER. I feel a little unhappy about it all myself. The trouble about being on the side of right, as one sees it, is that one sometimes finds oneself in the company of such very questionable allies. (*He sighs and rises*) Let's go and take our minds off it with television.

Lady Matheson (*rising*) Yes. Good idea. (*She moves towards the arch up* R) The newsreel will be nearly over now—but I think that dear Philip Harben is on. Such a pity I'll never have the chance of following any of his recipes. (*She passes Fowler*)

Fowler. I agree. One suffers the tortures of Tantalus, and yet the pleasure is intense. Isn't that what is today called masochism?

(Lady Matheson *exits up* R. Fowler *follows her off. The room is empty for a moment.*

The Major *tentatively appears at the open french windows. He peers cautiously into the room, and satisfying himself that it is empty, comes in. He goes quickly to the table up* C *and sees at once that the "West Hampshire Weekly News" is no longer where he left it. Frantically he rummages through the pile, and then begins to search the room. He stands a moment, in doubt.*

Sibyl *enters up* R. *As she sees the Major she stands stock still. He does not move, either*)

Major (*at length; with pathetic jauntiness*) Evening, Miss R.B. And how's the world with you, eh?

Sibyl (*standing above the easy chair*) Were you looking for mummy's paper?

Major (*standing above the sofa*) What? No, of course not. I've got the other copy.

Sibyl. Don't pretend any more, please. She's read it, you see.

Major. Oh.

(*There is a long pause*)

(*His shoulders droop*) Did she show it to you?

Sibyl. Yes.

Major. Oh.

Sibyl. And to all the others.

Major. Miss Cooper, too?

Sibyl. Mummy's gone to tell her.

(*The* Major *nods hopelessly, then moves to the settee* L *and sits*)

Major (*at length*) Oh—well—that's it, then, isn't it?

Sibyl. Yes.

Major. Oh, God! (*He stares at the floor*)

Sibyl (*looking steadily at him; passionately*) Why did you do it? Why did you do it?

Major. I don't know. I wish I could answer that. Why does any one do anything they shouldn't? Why do some people drink too much, and other people smoke fifty cigarettes a day? Because they can't stop it, I suppose.

Sibyl (*moving up* R *of the sofa*) Then this wasn't—then this wasn't—the first time?

Major. (*quietly*) No.

SIBYL (*half turning away*) It's horrible.

MAJOR. Yes, of course it is. I'm not trying to defend it. You wouldn't guess, I know, but ever since school I've always been scared to death of women.

(SIBYL *looks at him over her left shoulder*)

Of everyone, in a way, I suppose, but mostly of women. I had a bad time at school—which wasn't Wellington, of course—just a council school. Boys hate other boys to be timid and shy, and they gave it to me good and proper. My father despised me, too. He was a sergeant-major in the Black Watch. He made me join the Army, but I was always a bitter disappointment to him. He died before I got my commission. I only got that by a wangle. It wasn't difficult at the beginning of the war. But it meant everything to me, all the same. Being saluted, being called sir—I thought I'm someone now, a real person. Perhaps some woman might even . . . (*He breaks off*)

(SIBYL *turns away*)

But it didn't work. It never has worked. I'm made in a certain way, and I can't change it. It has to be the dark, you see, and strangers, because . . .

SIBYL (*holding her hands to her ears*) Stop, stop! I don't want to hear it. It makes me ill.

MAJOR (*quietly*) Yes. It would, of course. I should have known that. It was only that you'd asked me about why I did such things, and I wanted to talk to someone about it. I never have, you see, not in the whole of my life. (*He rises and moves up* L *of the sofa*) I'm sorry to have upset *you* of all people. (*He moves to the desk and picks up a book*)

SIBYL (*turning to him*) Why me, so especially? Why not the others?

(*The* MAJOR *moves to the french windows and looks at her over his left shoulder*)

MAJOR. Oh, I don't give a hang about the others. They'll all take it in their various ways, I suppose—but it won't mean much more to them than another bit of gossip to snort or snigger about. But it'll be different for you, Sibyl, and that makes me unhappy.

SIBYL. That's the first time you've ever called me Sibyl.

MAJOR. Is it? Well, there's not much point in all that Miss R. B. stuff now, it there?

SIBYL. What makes me so different from the others?

MAJOR (*crossing below the sofa to the fireplace*) Your being so scared of—well—what shall we call it—life? (*He picks up his pipe from the coffee table*) It sounds more respectable than the word which I know you hate. You and I are awfully alike, you know. That's why I suppose we've drifted so much together in this place.

Sibyl (*turning to him*) How can you say we're alike? *I* don't
go . . . (*She stops, unable to continue*)

Major (*looking at her*) I know you don't. You're not even
tempted, and never will be. You're very lucky. Or are you? Who's
to say, really? All I meant was that we're both of us frightened
of people, and yet we've somehow managed to forget our fright
when we've been in each other's company. (*He picks up his book
from the coffee table then searches on the mantelpiece*) Speaking
for myself, I'm grateful and always will be. Of course I can't
expect *you* to feel the same way now.

Sibyl. What are you doing?

Major. Getting my things together. Have you seen a tobacco
pouch anywhere?

Sibyl. It's here. (*She collects his pouch from the table up* c)

(*The* Major *moves to Sibyl and takes the pouch from her*)

Major (*with a wry smile*) Old Wellington colours.

Sibyl. Why have you told so many awful lies?

Major. I don't like myself as I am, I suppose, so I've had to
invent another person. It's not so harmful, really. We've all got
daydreams. Mine have gone a step further than most people's—
that's all. Quite often I've even managed to believe in the Major
myself. (*He starts*) Is that someone in the hall?

Sibyl (*listening*) No, I don't think so. Where will you go?

Major. I don't know. (*He moves up* r *of the sofa*) There's a
chap in London might put me up for a day or two. Only I don't
so awfully want to go there.

Sibyl. Why not?

Major (*after a slight pause*) Well—you see—it's rather a case of
birds of the feather.

Sibyl (*moving up* r *of the Major*) Don't go to him. You mustn't
go to him.

Major. I don't know where else.

Sibyl. Another hotel.

Major. It can't be Bournemouth or anywhere near here. It'll
have to be London, and I don't know anywhere in town I can
afford.

Sibyl. I'll lend you some money.

Major. You certainly won't.

Sibyl (*crossing above the Major to* l. *of the sofa*) I will. I have
some savings certificates. You can have those. I can get more, too,
if you need it.

Major (*holding her hand gently*) No, Sibyl. No. Thank you—
but no.

Sibyl. But you'll go to this man.

Major. No, I won't. I'll find somewhere else.

Sibyl. Where?

Major. Don't worry. I'll be all right.

(MISS COOPER *enters up* R *and stands above the chair* RC)

MISS COOPER (*brightly*) There you are, Major Pollock. Can I see you in my office a moment?

(SIBYL *turns away to the right corner of the desk and looks out of the french windows*)

MAJOR. We don't need to talk in your office, Miss Cooper. I know what you have to say. I'm leaving at once.
MISS COOPER. I see. That's your own choice, is it?
MAJOR. Of course.
MISS COOPER. Because I would like to make it perfectly plain to you that there's no question whatever of my requiring you to leave this hotel. If you want to stay on here you're at perfect liberty to do so. It's entirely a matter for you.

(*There is a pause*)

MAJOR. I see. That's good of you. But of course, I have to go.
MISS COOPER. I quite understand that you'd want to. I shan't charge the usual week's notice. When will you be going? Before dinner?
MAJOR. Of course.
MISS COOPER. Do you want me to help you find some place to stay until you can get settled?
MAJOR. I can hardly expect that, Miss Cooper.
MISS COOPER. Why on earth not? There are two hotels in London run by the Beauregard group. One is in West Kensington and the other in St John's Wood. They're both about the same price. Which would you prefer?
MAJOR (*after a pause*) West Kensington, I think.
MISS COOPER. I've got their card here somewhere. (*She moves to the mantelpiece and takes two cards from a small holder*) Yes, there's one here. (*She hands a card to the Major*) Would you like me to ring them up for you?
MAJOR. Thank you, but I think perhaps I'd better ring them myself. In case of—further trouble, I don't want to involve you more than I need. May I use the phone in your office?
MISS COOPER. Certainly. (*She moves to the fireplace and puts the second card on the mantelpiece*)
MAJOR. I'll pay you for the call, of course (*He goes to the arch up* R *and looks off to see if anyone is about in the hall*) Sibyl, if I don't have a chance of seeing you again, I'll write and say good-bye.

(*The* MAJOR *exits up* R)

MISS COOPER (*turning to Sibyl*) Your mother's gone up to dress for dinner, Miss Railton-Bell. She told me I'd find you in the writing-room lying down and I was to tell you that you can have your meal upstairs tonight, if you'd rather.

SIBYL. That's all right.

MISS COOPER (*moving above the armchair* RC; *sympathetically*) How are you feeling now?

SIBYL (*brusquely*) All right.

MISS COOPER (*moving below the table up* C; *quietly*) It there anything I can do to help you?

SIBYL (*with her back to Miss Cooper; angrily*) No. Nothing. And please don't say things like that. You'll make me feel bad again and I'll make a fool of myself. I feel well now. He's going, and that's good. I despise him.

MISS COOPER (*moving up* L *of the sofa*) Do you? I wonder if you should?

SIBYL (*over her shoulder*) He's a vile wicked man, and he's done a horrible, beastly thing. It's not the first time, either. He admits that.

MISS COOPER. I didn't think it was.

SIBYL (*looking out of the windows*) And yet you told him he could stay on in the hotel if he wanted to? That's wicked too?

MISS COOPER (*moving to Sibyl*) Then I suppose I *am* wicked, too. (*She puts her hand on Sibyl's arm*) Sibyl, dear . . .

SIBYL. Why is everyone calling me Sibyl this evening? Please stop. You'll only make me cry.

MISS COOPER. I don't mean to do that. I just mean to help you.

(SIBYL *breaks down suddenly, but now quietly and without hysteria*)

(*She puts an arm round Sibyl*) That's better. Much better.

SIBYL. It's so horrible.

MISS COOPER. I know it is. I'm very sorry for you.

SIBYL. He says we're alike—he and I.

MISS COOPER. Does he?

SIBYL. He says we're both scared of life and people and sex. There—I've said the word. He says I hate *saying* it even, and he's right. I do. What's the matter with me? There must be something the matter with me.

MISS COOPER. Nothing very much, I should say. Shall we sit down? (*She gently propels Sibyl to the sofa*)

(SIBYL *sits on the sofa at the left side.* MISS COOPER *sits up stage of Sibyl*)

SIBYL. I'm a freak, aren't I?

MISS COOPER (*in matter-of-fact tones*) I never know what that word means. If you mean you're different from other people, then, I suppose, you are a freak. But all human beings are a bit different from each other, aren't they? What a dull world it would be if they weren't.

SIBYL. I'd like to be ordinary.

MISS COOPER. I wouldn't know about that, dear. You see, I've never met an ordinary person. To me all people are extraordinary. I meet all sorts here, you know, in my job, and the one thing I've learnt in five years is that the word normal, applied to any human being, is utterly meaningless. In a sort of a way it's an insult to our Maker, don't you think, to suppose that He could possibly work to any set pattern?

SIBYL. I don't think mummy would agree with you.

MISS COOPER. I'm fairly sure she wouldn't. Tell me—when did your father die?

SIBYL. When I was seven.

MISS COOPER. Did you go to school?

SIBYL. No. Mummy said I was too delicate. I had a governess some of the time, but most of the time mummy taught me herself.

MISS COOPER. Yes. I see. And you've never really been away from her, have you?

SIBYL. Only when I had a job, for a bit. (*Proudly*) I was a sales-girl in a big shop in London—Jones & Jones. I sold lampshades. But I got ill, though, and had to leave.

MISS COOPER (*brightly*) What bad luck! Well, you must try again some day, mustn't you?

SIBYL. Mummy says no.

MISS COOPER. Mummy says no. Well then, you must try to get mummy to say yes, don't you think?

SIBYL. I don't know how.

MISS COOPER. I'll tell you how. By running off and getting a job on your own. She'll say yes quick enough then. (*She pats Sibyl's knee affectionately and rises*) I have my menus to do (*She moves up* R *of the sofa*)

SIBYL (*urgently*) Will he be all right, do you think?

MISS COOPER. The Major? I don't know. I hope so.

SIBYL. In spite of what he's done. I don't want anything bad to happen to him. I want him to be happy. Is it a nice hotel—this one in West Kensington?

MISS COOPER. Very nice.

SIBYL. Do you think he'll find a friend there? He told me just now that he'd always be grateful to me for making him forget how frightened he was of people.

MISS COOPER. He's helped you, too, hasn't he?

SIBYL. Yes.

MISS COOPER (*after a pause*) I hope he'll find a friend in the new hotel.

SIBYL. So do I. Oh, God, so do I!

(*The* MAJOR *enters up* R *and stands above the armchair* RC. MISS COOPER *turns to face him*)

MAJOR (*to Miss Cooper; quickly*) It's all right. I've fixed it. It might please you to know that I said *Mr* Pollock, and didn't have to mention your name, or this hotel. I must dash upstairs and pack now. (*He crosses to* R *of the sofa and holds out his hand to Sibyl*) Good-bye, Sibyl.

    (Sibyl *rises and, after a second's hesitation, takes his hand*)

Sibyl. Good-bye. (*She drops his hand and runs quickly to the arch up* R. *Without looking back*) God bless you.

    (Sibyl *exits up* R)

Major (*moving above the sofa to* L *of it*) Very upset?

    (Miss Cooper, *with her back to him, nods*)

That's the part I've hated most, you know. It's funny. She's rather an odd one—almost a case—she's got a child's mind and hardly makes sense sometimes—and yet she means quite a lot to me.

Miss Cooper (*turning to him*) I think you mean quite a lot to her.

Major. I did, I think. Not now, of course. It was the gallant ex-soldier she was fond of—not . . . (*He breaks off*) I told her the whole story about myself. I thought it right. There's just a chance she might understand it all a bit better one day. I'm afraid, though, she'll never get over it.

Miss Cooper (*half looking at him*) No. I don't suppose she will.

Major. One's apt to excuse oneself sometimes by saying: "Well, after all, what I do doesn't do anybody much harm." But one does, you see. That's not a thought I like. (*He takes some coins from his pocket, crosses and hands them to Miss Cooper*) Call to London, one and sixpence. Could you have a squint in the hall and see if anyone's around?

    (Miss Cooper *moves to the arch up* R *and glances off*)

Miss Cooper. Miss Meacham's at the telephone.
Major. Damn!
Miss Cooper (*moving up* R *of the sofa*) What train are you catching?
Major. Seven forty-five.
Miss Cooper. You've got time.
Major (*moving up* L *of the sofa*) I've got a tremendous lot of packing to do. Four years, you know. Hellish business. I'm dreading the first few days in a new place. I mean dreading, you know —literally trembling with funk at the thought of meeting new people. The trouble is I'll probably be forced by sheer terror to take refuge in all that Major stuff again.
Miss Cooper. Try not to.
Major. Oh, I'll try all right. I'll try. I only hope I'll succeed. (*He crosses to the arch up* R *and looks cautiously off*) Still there. Damn! (*He moves above the armchair* RC) Thank you for being so kind. God knows why you have been. I don't deserve it—but I'm grateful. Very grateful.

MISS COOPER. That's all right.

MAJOR. You're an odd fish, you know, if you don't mind my saying so. A good deal more goes on behind that calm managerial front of yours than anyone would imagine. Has something bad ever happened to you?

MISS COOPER. Yes.

MAJOR. Very bad?

MISS COOPER. I've got over it.

MAJOR. What was it?

MISS COOPER. I loved a man who loved somebody else.

MAJOR. Still love him?

MISS COOPER. Oh, yes. I always will.

MAJOR. Any hope?

MISS COOPER (*cheerfully*) No. None at all.

MAJOR. Why so cheerful about it?

MISS COOPER. Because there's no point in being anything else. I've settled for the situation, you see, and it's surprising how cheerful one can be when one gives up hope. I've still got the memory, you see, which is a very pleasant one—all things considered.

MAJOR (*nodding*) I see. Quite the philosopher, what? (*To himself*) I must give up saying "what". Well, Meacham or no Meacham, I'm going to make a dash for it, or I'll miss that train.

(*He moves to the arch up* R)

MISS COOPER. Why don't you stay?

MAJOR (*turning; increduously*) Stay? In the hotel, you mean?

MISS COOPER. You say you dread the new hotel.

MAJOR. I dread this one a damn sight more now.

MISS COOPER. Yes, I expect you do. But at least you couldn't be forced by terror into any more Major stuff, could you?

(*There is a pause*)

MAJOR. I might be forced into something a good deal more— conclusive—cleaning my old service revolver, perhaps—you know the form—making a nasty mess on one of your carpets and an ugly scandal in your hotel.

MISS COOPER (*lightly*) I'd take the risk if you would.

MAJOR. My dear Miss Cooper, I'm far too much of a coward to stay on here now. Far too much.

MISS COOPER. I see. Pity. I just thought it would be so nice if you could prove to yourself that you weren't.

(*There is a pause*)

MAJOR (*at length*) You're thinking of her, too, of course, aren't you?

MISS COOPER. Yes.

MAJOR. Reinstate the gallant ex-soldier in her eyes?

MISS COOPER. That's right.

Major. Make her think she's helped me find my soul and all
that.

Miss Cooper. Yes.

(There is a pause)

Major *(with an eventual sigh)* Not a hope. Not a hope in the
whole wide, blinking world. I know my form, you see.

Miss Cooper. I wonder if you do.

Major *(sadly)* Oh, I do. I do, only too well. Thanks for trying
anyway. *(He looks cautiously off R)* Coast's clear. *(He turns and
looks at Miss Cooper for a long time)*

(Miss Cooper *stares back steadily at the Major*)

(At length) There's a nine something train, isn't there?

Miss Cooper. Nine thirty-two.

*(There is another pause as the Major looks at Miss Cooper
in doubt, then he gives a shamefaced smile)*

Major. I expect I'll still catch the seven forty-five.

The Major exits up R and the lights dim as—

the Curtain falls

SCENE II

SCENE—*The dining-room. Dinner time.*

When the CURTAIN *rises, dinner is in full swing. The table by the window is occupied by* CHARLES *and* JEAN, *much interested in each other, and totally oblivious of everyone else. They are on the sweet course. The table down* LC *is unoccupied and unlaid.* MISS MEACHAM *is at her usual table. She has finished her soup and is absorbed in "Racing Up To Date".* FOWLER *is at his table eating his sweet.* LADY MATHESON *is down* R, *eating her sweet.* MRS RAILTON-BELL *is seated above the table down* RC *with* SIBYL R *of it. They are eating their meat course. The table up* C *is occupied by a young pair of* CASUALS *who are on their sweet course. Conversation is general, which means, more precisely, that the two* CASUALS *are murmuring together,* CHARLES *and* JEAN *are arguing, and* MRS RAILTON-BELL *is talking to Sibyl.* MABEL *is hovering over Miss Meacham, with her tray and a plate of fricassee.*

MABEL (*heard above the background*) Were you the fricassee or the cambridge steak?

MISS MEACHAM. What? Oh, it doesn't matter. Both are uneatable.

MABEL. What about the cold chicken, then?

MISS MEACHAM. Cold chicken? We haven't had the hot yet.

MABEL. If I were you I'd have the fricasee. It's all right. It's rabbit.

MISS MEACHAM. The fricassee, then.

FOWLER. Any cheese, Mabel?

MABEL. No, cheese off.

FOWLER. Never any cheese.

(MABEL *serves Miss Meacham and stumps out to the kitchen.* MRS RAILTON-BELL *leans across to Lady Matheson*)

MRS RAILTON-BELL. Gladys, dear, I believe there's a new game on television tonight.

LADY MATHESON. Yes, I know, dear. I read all about it in the *Radio Times*. It sounds quite fascinating—I shall certainly see it next week.

MRS RAILTON-BELL. Why not tonight, dear?

LADY MATHESON. I felt too tired. I'm going to go to bed directly after dinner.

MRS RAILTON-BELL. Of course. (*She lowers her voice*) What a really nerve-racking day it's been, hasn't it? I don't suppose any of us will ever forget it. Ever. I feel utterly shattered, myself. Anyway, thank heavens it's all over and done with now. (*To Sibyl*) ~~Pass the sauce, dear.~~

JEAN (*to Charles*) Just because we saw that awful film at the *Odeon* . . .

(*The* MAJOR *enters up* LC. LADY MATHESON'*s face freezes when she sees the Major.* MRS RAILTON-BELL *turns quickly, sees him and freezes, too. The conversation dies suddenly to silence, save for the murmuring from the* CASUALS. *The* MAJOR *moves slowly to the table down* LC, *and sits, without looking right or left. He switches on his table lamp. The silence continues and even seems to affect the two* CASUALS, *who, by now, have stopped talking.*

DOREEN *enters from the kitchen and sees the Major. She breaks the silence by calling through the kitchen door*)

DOREEN. Mabel—Number Seven's in. You said he was out.

MABEL (*off; calling*) Well, that's what Joe said. Joe said he was leaving before dinner.

DOREEN (*moving to* R *of the Major*) Sorry, Major. There's been a muddle. I'll lay your table right away.

(DOREEN *exits to the kitchen. The* GIRL CASUAL *laughs.*

DOREEN *re-enters. She carries a tray of cutlery for the Major's table*)

(*She moves to* R *of the Major and sets out the cutlery*) What would you like? The fricassee's nice. Soup first?

MAJOR. No, thank you.

DOREEN (*finishing the table*) There we are. All cosy now.

(DOREEN *exits to the kitchen.* SIBYL *is staring at the* MAJOR, *but he does not meet her eyes. He is looking down at his table, as is everyone else, aware of his presence, save* SIBYL *and* MRS RAILTON-BELL, *who is glaring furiously in turn at him and at the others. Silence reigns, broken suddenly by a rather nervously high-pitched greeting from* CHARLES)

CHARLES (*to the Major*) Good evening.

MAJOR (*murmuring*) Good evening.

(JEAN *glares furiously at Charles.* MRS RAILTON-BELL *turns fully round in her chair in an attempt to paralyse Charles into silence*)

CHARLES. Clouding over a bit, isn't it? I'm afraid we may get rain later.

MAJOR. Yes, I'm afraid we may.

MISS MEACHAM. We need it. This hard going's murder on form. (*To the Major*) You know Newmarket, Major, don't you?

MAJOR. No, I don't.

MISS MEACHAM. But I remember your saying . . . (*She gets it*) Oh, I see. Well, it's a very tricky course in hard going. Still, if they get some rain up there tomorrow, I think I'll be able to give you a winner on Tuesday.

MAJOR. I may not be here on Tuesday.

MISS MEACHAM. Oh, really? All right. Leave me your address then, and I'll wire it to you. I'll need the money for the wire though.

MAJOR. Thank you. That's very kind of you.

MISS MEACHAM. You won't think it so kind of me if it loses. (*She goes back to her book*)

(MISS COOPER *enters from the kitchen*)

MISS COOPER (*brightly*) Good evening, Mrs Railton-Bell. Good evening, Lady Matheson. (*She moves to* R *of the Major*) Good evening, Mr Pollock. (*The "Mr" is barely distinguishable from "Major", and her voice is as brightly "managerial" to him as to the others*) I hear they didn't lay your table tonight. I'm so sorry.

MAJOR. Quite all right.

MISS COOPER. I recommend the fricassee. It's really awfully good.

MAJOR. I've ordered it.

MISS COOPER. Good, I'm so glad. (*She turns and passes on up stage*) Good evening, Mr and Mrs Stratton. Everything all right?

(CHARLES *and* JEAN *nod and smile*)

Splendid.

(MISS COOPER *bows rather less warmly to the Casuals, and exits up* LC. MRS RAILTON-BELL *pretends to feel an imaginary draught*)

MRS RAILTON-BELL (*to LadyMatheson*) It's very cold in here suddenly, don't you think, dear?

(LADY MATHESON *nods, nervously*)

I think I'll turn my chair round a bit, and get out of the draught. (*She turns her chair, turning her back neatly on the Major*)

(FOWLER *rises quietly and moves toward the door up* LC. *To do this he has to pass the Major. A step or so past him, he hesitates, then looks back, nods and smiles*)

FOWLER (*to the Major*) Good evening.

(MRS RAILTON-BELL *has to twist her head sharply round in order to allow her eyes to confirm this shameful betrayal*)

MAJOR. Good evening.

FOWLER. Hampshire did pretty well today, did you see? Three hundred and eighty-odd for five.

MAJOR. Very good.
FOWLER. I wish they had more bowling. Well . . .

(FOWLER *smiles vaguely then exits up* LC. *There is an audible and outraged "Well!" from* MRS RAILTON-BELL. *Silence falls again. Suddenly and by an accident, the* MAJOR's *and* LADY MATHESON's *eyes meeet. Automatically she inclines her head and gives him a slight smile. The* MAJOR *returns the salute.* LADY MATHESON, *who has genuinely acted from instinct, looks startled. Then she apparently decides to be as well hanged for a sheep as a lamb)*

LADY MATHESON (*suddenly very bold and in a loud voice*) I advise the apple charlotte. It's very good.
MAJOR. Thank you. I'll have that.

(LADY MATHESON *is instantly conscience-stricken at what she has done, and hangs her head over the apple charlotte, eating feverishly. She refuses to look at* MRS RAILTON-BELL, *who is staring at her with wide, unbelieving and furious eyes.* MRS RAILTON-BELL, *getting no response from Lady Matheson, deliberately folds her napkin and rises)*

MRS RAILTON-BELL (*quietly*) Come, Sibyl.
SIBYL (*equally quietly*) I haven't finished yet, Mummy.
MRS RAILTON-BELL (*looking puzzled at this unaccustomed response*) It doesn't matter, dear. Come into the lounge.

(SIBYL *makes no move to rise. She stares up at her mother. There is a pause)*

SIBYL. No, Mummy.

(*There is a pause*)

MRS RAILTON-BELL (*sharply*) Sibyl, come with me at once.
SIBYL (*with quiet firmness*) No, Mummy. I'm going to stay in the dining-room and finish my dinner.

(MRS RAILTON-BELL *hesitates, plainly meditating various courses of action. Finally she decides on the only really possible course left to her, the dignified exit. She moves towards the door up* LC, *but before she reaches it,* SIBYL *has spoken to the Major)*

There's a new moon tonight, you know. We must all go and look for it afterwards.
MAJOR. Yes. We must.

(DOREEN *bustles in from the kitchen. She carries a tray with fricassee and vegetables for the Major.*
MRS RAILTON-BELL, *her world crumbling, exits up* LC)

DOREEN (*moving to* R *of the Major*) Sorry it's been so long. You're a bit late, you see. (*She serves the Major*)

MAJOR. Yes. My fault.

DOREEN. What's the matter with you tonight? You always say "*mea culpa*". (*She beats her breast in imitation of an obvious Major bon mot*)

MAJOR. Do I? Well—they both mean the same, don't they?

DOREEN. I suppose so. (*Finishing the serving*) There you are. Now what about breakfast?

MAJOR. Breakfast?

DOREEN. Joe got it wrong about your going, didn't he?

(*There is a pause.* SIBYL *looks steadily at the* MAJOR, *who now raises his eyes from his plate and meets her glance*)

MAJOR (*quietly*) Yes, he did.

DOREEN. That's good. Breakfast usual time, then?

MAJOR. Yes, Doreen. Breakfast usual time.

DOREEN *exits to the kitchen. The* MAJOR *eats his fricassee.* SIBYL *continues with her meal. A decorous silence, broken only by the renewed murmur of the* CASUALS, *reigns once more, and the dining-room of the Beauregard Private Hotel no longer gives any sign of the battle that has just been fought and won between its four, bare walls.*

CURTAIN

FURNITURE AND PROPERTY PLOT

TABLE BY THE WINDOW

SCENE I

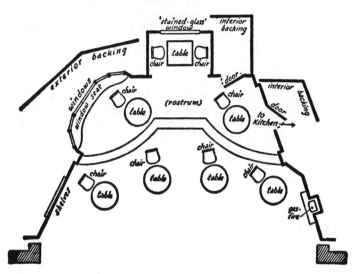

On stage: Table (down R) *On it:* white cloth, napkin in ring, glass, jug of water, sauce bottle, table lamp, vase of flowers, cruet, menu, large knife and fork, small knife, dessert spoon and fork, roll on side plate, soup plate, soup spoon

Table (down RC) *On it:* white cloth, napkin in ring, cruet, menu, table lamp, wine glass, ½ bottle Graves, side plate, dessert spoon and fork, small knife, plate of sweet—turnover, small plate with apple, flowers

Table (down LC) *On it:* white cloth, napkin and ring, glass, jug of water, cruet, menu, table lamp, flowers, soup spoon, large knife and fork, dessert spoon and fork, small knife, side plate, roll, ashtray

Table (down L) *On it:* white cloth, cruet, menu, napkin in ring, bottle of Vichy water, tumbler, sauce, table lamp, flowers, soup spoon, large knife and fork, small knife, dessert spoon and fork, side plate, roll, plate of soup, ashtray

Table (up RC) *On it:* white cloth, table lamp, napkin in ring, flowers, glass, soup spoon, large knife and fork, dessert spoon and fork, small knife, side plate, ashtray, cruet, menu, roll on side plate

Table (up LC) *On it:* white cloth, table lamp, flowers, napkin in ring, glass, jug of water, Worcester sauce, soup spoon, large knife and fork, small knife, dessert spoon and fork, side plate, roll, plate of soup, racing book, cruet, menu

Table (up C) *On it:* white cloth, table lamp, flowers, 2 napkins in rings, 2 dessert spoons and forks, 2 side plates, 2 jellies, 2 glasses, 1 bottle beer, 1 bottle Guinness, 2 books

8 dining chairs

On alcove shelves: small urn, decorative plates, packet charcoal biscuits, bottle of sauce, jars of marmalade and pickles, bottles of Lucozade, barley water, and Vichy water, packets of Energen and Bemax

On mantelpiece: 2 vases

Pair of net curtains

Pair chintz curtains

Doors closed

Window curtains closed

Table lamps on

Off stage: Tray. *On it:* goulash for Miss Meacham, medaillon for Lady Matheson, 2 dishes vegetables (MABEL)

Tray. *On it:* plate of tongue and salad (DOREEN)

Tray. *On it:* plate with turnover for Miss Meacham (MABEL)

Tray. *On it:* plate of goulash, dish of vegetables (MABEL)

Tray. *On it:* plate of turnover for Lady Matheson (MABEL)

Tray. *On it:* plate of turnover for Anne (MABEL)

Tray. *On it:* plate of soup for John (DOREEN)

Tray. *On it:* medaillon and dish of vegetables for John (DOREEN)

Personal: FOWLER: small change

JOHN: watch

ANNE: handbag. *In it:* compact

SCENE II

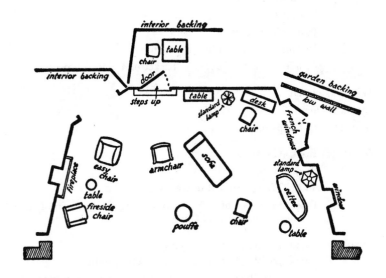

On stage: Sofa. *On it:* cushions

Chair (LC) *On it:* cushion

Armchair (RC) *On it:* cushion

Easy chair

Fireside chair (down R) *On it:* cushion
Under it: Lady Matheson's spectacles

Coffee table. *On it:* ashtray

Settee (L)

2 standard lamps

Occasional table (down L) *On it:* ashtray

Table (up C) *On it:* magazines, ashtray

Desk. *On it:* blotter, inkstand, pens, ashtray, hotel paper, envelopes, piece of crumpled paper

Waste-paper basket

Pouffe

Desk chair

Club fender

Gas fire
Mirror over mantelpiece
On mantelpiece: candlesticks, vases
Over fireplace: 2 electric wall-brackets
Pictures on walls
Carpet on floor
Pair chintz curtains
In hall backing: radiator, picture
In window alcove down L: basket of artificial flowers

Windows closed
Curtains closed
Brackets and lamps on

Off stage: Book (CHARLES)
Book (JEAN)
Radio Times (MRS RAILTON-BELL)
Tray. *On it:* pot of coffee, cup, saucer, spoon, basin of sugar, jug of milk (MISS COOPER)

Personal: CHARLES: pencil, handkerchief
JOHN: packet of cork-tipped cigarettes, lighter
ANNE: handbag. *In it:* gold cigarette case with cigarettes, lighter, cigarette holder, key

SCENE III

On stage: Table (down R) *On it:* white cloth, napkin, cruet, flowers, table lamp, menu

Table (down RC) *On it:* white cloth, napkin, flowers, table lamp, cruet

Table (down LC) *On it:* white cloth, table lamp, flowers

Table (down L) *On it:* white cloth, napkin, cruet, flowers, table lamp

Table (up RC) *On it:* white cloth, napkin, table lamp, cruet, ashtray

Table (up LC) *On it:* white cloth, napkin in ring, pot of tea, jug of milk, basin of sugar, tea cup and saucer, spoon, jar of marmalade, 1 piece of toast on plate, butter in dish, small knife, racing book, flowers, morning paper

Table (up C) *On it:* white cloth, 2 napkins, 2 side plates, 2 knives, toast on side plates, butter, jar of marmalade, pot of tea, jug of milk, basin of sugar, 2 cups and saucers, 2 spoons, 2 books, table lamp, flowers

Other dressing as before

Doors closed

Window curtains open

Table lamps off

Off stage: Tray. *On it:* pot of tea, jug of milk, basin of sugar, tea-cup, saucer, spoon, plate of digestive biscuits (DOREEN)

Tray. *On it:* 2 plates digestive biscuits (DOREEN)

Tray. *On it:* pot of coffee, cup, saucer, spoon (DOREEN)

Personal: JOHN: case with cigarettes, lighter

ANNE: handkerchief

TABLE NUMBER SEVEN

SCENE I

Lounge setting and furniture as before

Set: On table up C: vase of flowers, copy of *West Hampshire Weekly News,* tobacco pouch

On desk: library book

In hearth: empty cigarette packet

On mantelpiece: hotel cards

Change artificial flowers down L to hydrangeas

French windows open

Window curtains open

Fire off

Brackets and lamps off

Off stage: Large medical treatise (CHARLES)

Pram. *In it:* doll as baby, blanket (JEAN)

2 library books (MAJOR)

Letter (FOWLER)

West Hampshire Weekly News (MISS COOPER)

Vase of flowers (MISS COOPER)

Book and spectacles (SIBYL)

Book and spectacle case (SIBYL)

Baby nightdress, bodkin, ribbon (JEAN)

Personal: MAJOR: pipe, pouch of tobacco, matches, coins

MRS RAILTON-BELL: handbag

LADY MATHESON: handbag. *In it:* spectacles

CHARLES: handkerchief

SCENE II

On stage: Table (down RC) *On it:* white cloth, napkin in ring, glass, jug of water, cruet, menu, flowers, table lamp, dessert spoon and fork, small knife, side plate, apple charlotte on plate

Table (down R) *On it:* white cloth, table lamp, flowers, menu, cruet, 2 napkins in rings, 1 wine glass, 1 tumbler, 2 bottles wine, 2 plates of fricassee, 2 side plates, 2 large knives, 2 small knives, 2 large forks, 2 small forks, 2 dessert spoons, 2 rolls, sauce

Table (down LC) *On it:* White cloth, table lamp, cruet, napkin in ring, menu (lamp unlit)

Table (down L) *On it:* white cloth, table lamp, flowers, cruet, menu, side plate, dessert spoon and fork, napkin in ring, tumbler, Vichy water, plate of banana mashed, sauce

Table (up RC) *On it:* white cloth, 2 napkins, 2 side plates and rolls, 2 tumblers, cruet, table lamp, menu, flowers, 2 dessert spoons and forks, 2 small knives, 2 plates of sweet (jelly or apple purée) jug of water

Table (up LC) *On it:* white cloth, table lamp, cruet, flowers, menu, napkin, side plate, roll, soup spoon, large knife and fork, dessert spoon and fork, small knife, plate of soup, Worcester sauce

Table (up C) *On it:* white cloth, table lamp, flowers, menu, 2 napkins, 2 side plates, 2 dessert spoons and forks, 2 glasses, jug of water, 2 plates of apple or jelly

Set: Extra chair at table down RC

Extra chair at table up RC

New flowers

Flowers in vases on mantelpiece

Other dressing as before

Doors closed

Window curtains closed

Table lamps on except lamp on table down LC

Off stage: Tray. *On it:* plate of fricassee for Mrs Meacham (MABEL)

Tray. *On it:* soup spoon, large knife and fork, small knife, dessert spoon and fork, small plate with roll, tumbler (DOREEN)

Tray. *On it:* plate of fricassee and dish of vegetables for the Major (DOREEN)

LIGHTING PLOT

TABLE BY THE WINDOW

Property fittings required: 7 small table lamps with pink shades, 2 standard lamps, 2 wall brackets

SCENE I. Interior. A hotel dining-room. Night

THE MAIN ACTING AREAS are at 7 tables, R, RC, up RC, up C, up LC, LC and L

THE APPARENT SOURCES OF LIGHT are table lamps on the tables

To open: Table lamps on
Strip outside door up L, on
Strip outside door up LC, on

Cue 1 At end of scene (Page 13)
Quick dim of all lights except table-lamps, to BLACK-OUT

SCENE II. Interior. A hotel lounge. Night

THE MAIN ACTING AREAS are at sofa LC, a chair RC and at a fireplace R

THE APPARENT SOURCES OF LIGHT are wall-brackets over the fireplace R and standard lamps L and up LC

To open: Lamps and brackets, on
Blue outside french windows up L
Strip outside arch up RC, on
Strip outside door up RC, on

Cue 2 At end of scene (Page 35)
Quick dim of all lights to BLACK-OUT

SCENE III. The dining-room. A winter's morning

THE APPARENT SOURCE OF LIGHT is a large window R

To open: Daylight outside window
Table lamps, off
Strip outside door up L, on
Strip outside door up LC, on

No cues

TABLE NUMBER SEVEN

SCENE I. The lounge. A summer's day

THE APPARENT SOURCE OF LIGHT is the french windows up L.

To open: Effect of bright sunlight

Lamps and brackets, off

Strip outside arch up R, on

Strip outside door up RC, on

Cue 3   At end of scene   (Page 81)
Quick dim of all lights to BLACK-OUT

SCENE II. The dining-room. Night

To open: Table lamps, on, *except* lamp on table down LC

Strip outside door up L, on

Strip outside door LC, on

Cue 4   The MAJOR switches on the table lamp down LC   (Page 83)
Snap in table lamp on table down LC
Bring up lights to cover

MADE AND PRINTED IN GREAT BRITAIN BY
LATIMER TREND & COMPANY LTD PLYMOUTH